Hebrew with Joy!

Learn Simple Hebrew with the Scriptures

Teacher's Guide

Joy Carroll

Hebrew with Joy!: Teacher's Guide

©2019 by SimkhaPress
ISBN: 978-1-7333230-0-0

Unless otherwise noted, Scriptures are from The Holy Bible, Tree of Life Version (TLV)
© 2011, 2012, 2013, 2014 & 2015 by the Messianic Jewish Family Bible Society.

Scripture quotations marked NIV are taken from The Holy Bible, New International Version® NIV® Copyright © 1973, 1978, 1984, 2011 by Biblica, Inc.™ Used by permission.

All rights reserved. No part of this publication may be reproduced, stored or transmitted in any form or by any means, including photocopying, recording, or other technology, without the written permission of the publisher.

Paleo-Hebrew for "shalom" used with permission by Dr. I Suuquina
http://www.indigenousmessengers.com

The websites cited in this book were active at time of publishing. There is no guarantee that they will continue to be available in the future.

For supplemental products for use with this book, visit: http://HebrewWithJoy.com

Rev. Date: 2-20

הֹד֣וּ לַיהוָ֣ה כִּי־ט֑וֹב כִּ֖י לְעוֹלָ֣ם חַסְדּֽוֹ׃

Psalm 107:1 *Praise ADONAI, for He is good,*
for His lovingkindness endures forever.

Hebrew with Joy! (HWJ) is dedicated to my husband, Russ,
who has always encouraged me to follow my dreams!

Todah Rabah (thanks very much) to:
HWJ Prayer Team: your faithfulness to pray for me through
this project provided the encouragement, inspiration,
strength and energy to complete HWJ
Graphic Designer: our wonderful daughter, Becca Kendall
HWJ Editing Team:
Pam Neilson, Jackie Newman, Erin Miskey, Natasha Cinkosky,
Juliet Rizzo, Gaylyn Williams, Adam Haeffner, Cecilia Mikolajczak,
Alleluyah Williams, Marion Torrez
Proofing: Linda Harris
Website Support: Joshua Morgan, Pat Cohen, Deb Wiley
Author Photo: Randie Ide
Publishing Support: Gordon Saunders, Greg Wiley
Audio Editor: Daveed Vogt
Software Support: Jeremy Begley
Inspiration Launch Team: Margie Wood, Esh Gray
Marketing: Olenka Nakka

A very special thanks to our congregation, Etz Khayim, for supporting and
encouraging my Hebrew classes over the years.

Todah rabah (thanks so much) <u>to all of my Hebrew students</u>, who,
for the past six years, have contributed ideas and suggestions
to make this book more complete and user-friendly!

Table of Contents

Introduction 7
Course Syllabus 9
Alef Bet Song 13
Lesson 1 ב שׁ שׂ ת 15
Lesson 2 ל מ ם 21
Lesson 3 ר י ה 27
Lesson 4 נ ן ע א 33
Lesson 5 כ ך ד ח 39
Lesson 6 ד ב ו 49
Lesson 7 פּ ז צ ץ 55
Lesson 8 פ ף ק כ 61
Lesson 9 שׁ ס ט ג 69
Lesson 10   Reading Scriptures 79
Lesson Fill-Ins 94
Hebrew Letters 96
Hebrew Vowels 98
Hebrew Phrases 100
Hebrew Resources 101
Scriptural and Cultural Treasures Index 103
Hebrew Dictionary 105
Teacher Resources **108**
Supply List **109**
Shalom Chaverim - 3 pages **111**
Graduation Certificate **117**

Notice new teacher sections above in bold

Introduction

Encourage students to read this page before using the book.

Shalom and welcome to **Hebrew with Joy!**
This book is the first step for Hebrew beginners who have a desire to learn the Holy Language of the Living God. Learning to read the original Hebrew of the Bible brings a greater understanding of the heart of Adonai (God.)

Audio files which record the Hebrew for each lesson are available at no charge. The files can be accessed on our website: https://hebrewwithjoy.com/audio-files/   Password: listen

Video Lesson Files can be used to supplement this book and reinforce what you have learned. These lessons can be helpful whether teaching individuals, families, home school, bible study or other groups. The videos can be purchased at:
https://hebrewwithjoy.com/hebrew-with-joy-video-lessons/

Pronunciation: Hebrew with Joy! teaches the *Sephardic* form of pronunciation to honor the standard pronunciation used in Israel.

Lesson 1 includes a teacher point on Ashkenazi pronunciation.

English Transliterations and Accented Syllables in this book are based on the following chart:

English Transliteration Sounds			
a	"a" as in <u>a</u>ll	kh	"ch" as in Ba<u>ch</u>
e	"e" as in <u>e</u>gg	ay	"ay" as is l<u>ay</u>
ee	"ee" as in f<u>ee</u>t	ai	"i" as in p<u>ie</u>
o	"o" as in <u>o</u>ver	oy	"oy" as in b<u>oy</u>
oo	"oo" as in t<u>oo</u>	ooey	"ooey" as in g<u>ooey</u>
CAPITAL letters show the accented syllable in a word as in "sha-LOM"			
If the accent is *not* on the last syllable, it will be **BOLD** as in "**E**-rev"			

Before Lesson 1, review this chart with your class to practice English transliterations.

Suggestions for Students:

- Try to study with a partner. The accountability and interaction will aid in learning.
- Create your own flashcards as each new letter, vowel, root and key word is introduced. Then practice every day!
- Try *not* to write the Hebrew transliterations (English sounds) above the Hebrew in the book! This will slow down the learning process.
- If this is your first Hebrew class, practice writing in block letters. If you know the Alef-Bet already, take the challenge to learn script, which is the standard of writing in Israel. (Refer to the Hebrew Letter pages in the Appendix)
- After each lesson is taught, use the learning activity that goes with the lesson. It will reinforce the materials in a fun, up-beat way.
- Listen to the audio files between class sessions to reinforce the new letter and vowel sounds as you practice your pronunciation.
- Have fun as you learn the language of God!

Suggestions for Teachers:

This page has the most important general suggestions for teachers – take the time to read and digest each point!

- Encourage students to make their own flashcards as each new letter, vowel, root and key word is introduced. (Students can purchase notecards and markers before class or the teacher can supply them.)

- Try to discourage students from writing the Hebrew transliterations (English sounds) above the Hebrew in the book! This will slow down the learning process.

- Although both block and script handwriting are included in each lesson, brand new Hebrew students should write in block to reinforce the new letters. The script is included as an extra challenge for students who already know the Alef Bet.

- Allow students to work as partners as much as possible. For example, partners can practice reading a line of letter combinations to each other before speaking out loud to the entire class. Be sure to call on all students to read out loud.

- When a student is reading out loud and makes a mistake, *first* ask the student to try the word again. Then, if they still struggle, ask if another student can help. As a *last* resort, the teacher pronounces the word.

- After each lesson is taught, use the learning activity that goes with the lesson. It will reinforce the materials in a fun, up-beat way.

- Answers to Lesson Exercises can be found on this web page:

    HebrewWithJoy.com/HWJ-exercise-answers   Password: answers

- Encourage students to listen to the audio files between class sessions. This will especially help the audio learners.

- **Video Lesson Files** can also be used as a teaching tool. They can be ordered at: https://hebrewwithjoy.com/hebrew-with-joy-video-lessons/

More Teacher Suggestions:

- **Teacher PowerPoint** slide shows are available for all HWJ Lessons and can be ordered at www.HebrewWithJoy.com.
- **Use Hebrew phrases as you teach** (see Hebrew Phrases in Appendix.)
- Classes meeting 2 days per week result in the best Hebrew retention.
- Offer a reward (Ex. small pieces of chocolate) to those who volunteer in class and to those who win the games.
- **CHAIN DRILL:** Try to set up student tables in a "U" shape. Student 1 recites first conversational phrase, student 2 answers. Then Student 2 turns to Student 3 and they practice together, then Student 3 turns to Student 4 and so on until all students have practiced.
- **LONG WORDS:** If a word has many syllables (Ex. l-heet-ra-OT), start from the back to break it down! Start with "OT" and have them repeat. Then say "ra-OT", repeat, then "heet-ra-OT", repeat, then "l-heet-ra-OT", repeat. It works!
- Syllable lines are also helpful for long words – (see Lesson 10.)
- For **board games**, scan the games and print on colored cardstock.

Course Syllabus

Encourage students to review this page often at home as it summarizes all information taught in each lesson

New Key Word		New Root		New Vowels	New Letters	#
Sabbath	שַׁבָּת	rest, stop	שׁ.ב.ת	ָ ַ	שׁ ב ת	1
peace	שָׁלוֹם	completion, wholeness	שׁ.ל.ם	וֹ	ל מ ם	2
instruction	תּוֹרָה	hit the mark	י.ר.ה	ֱ ֲ ֳ	ה ר י	3
hear	שְׁמַע	hear and obey	שׁ.מ.ע	ְ ֶ ֵ	נ ן ע א	4
blessed	בָּרוּךְ	bless, kneel	ב.ר.ך	וּ ֻ	כ ד ח	5
love	אַהֲבָה	love	א.ה.ב	ַ ֲ	ד ב ו	6
life	חַיִּים	live	ח.י.ה	יִ	צ ץ פ ז	7
holy	קָדוֹשׁ	holy	ק.ד.ש	ָ	פ ף כ ק	8
joy	שִׂמְחָה	joyful	שׂ.מ.ח	וִ וִ	ט ג שׂ ס	9
Reading Scriptures						10

HWJ Teacher's Guide   Course Syllabus

**Please complete this page without looking up any answers.
This evaluates your Hebrew knowledge before the class.

> During the first class, make sure all students fill out this Pre-Quiz – CLOSED BOOK! Refer to it after class 5 and 10 so students can see their progress.

Name: _____

Date: _____

Pre-Quiz

A. Was this your first Hebrew class? _____

B. Match the letters to their sounds:

ע _3_   1. d

צ _6_   2. r

פּ _7_   3. silent

ר _2_   4. s

ק _5_   5. k

ד _1_   6. ts

ס _4_   7. p

C. Match the sounds:

תָ _4_   1. too

תוֹ _5_   2. tee

תַ _2_   3. tie

תוּ _1_   4. tah

תִי _3_   5. toe

תִ _7_   6. teh

תֵ _6_   7. tay

D. Match the words:

שְׁמַע _4_   1. life

קָדוֹשׁ _3_   2. blessed

חַיִּים _1_   3. holy

בָּרוּךְ _2_   4. hear

E. Match the roots:

שׂ.מ.ח _3_   1. hit the mark

י.ר.ה _1_   2. love

שׁ.ב.ת _4_   3. joy

א.ה.ב _2_   4. rest/stop

E. Write in Hebrew: Sabbath Peace _____ שַׁבָּת שָׁלוֹם! _____

Alef Bet Song

By Debbie Friedman

Search Online: Debbie Friedman Alef Bet Video

Please note: some letter names have been changed to match the letter sounds

א	ב	ב
A-lef	Bet	Vet

ג ד ה
GI-mel **DA**-let Hay

ו ז ח ט
Vav **ZA**-yin Khet Tet

י כ כ
Yud Khaf Kaf

ל מ נ
LA-med Mem Nun

ס ע פ פ
SA-mekh **A**-yin Pay Fay

צ ק ר
TSA-dee Koof Raysh

ש שׂ ת
Shin Sin Tav

> *Find the Alef Bet song on the internet and sing it with your students OR lead the students yourself.*
>
> *This is a beloved song for young beginners. You may want to point out that some of the letter names have been changed to make it easier for young ones to remember the letter sounds. Ex. The Shin has 2 sounds. If the dot is on the right, it has the "sh" sound. If the dot is on the left, the "s" sound.*
>
> *In this song, for younger students, the names are "shin" and "sin" to make it easier to remember.*

Lesson 1 שׁ ת ב

Israeli Greeting
Hello! My name is _____.   shalom! sh-mee _____.

Use the Chain Drill (see Teacher Introduction.)

A - Letters

Focus on the visual reminders!

Sound	Name	Letter	
"b" as in **b**ar (Bet has a **b**ottom **b**ar)	Bet (with a middle dot)	בּ	A1
"t" as in **t**oe (Tav has a toe)	Tav	ת	A2
"sh" as in **sh**ine	Shin (dot on top right)	שׁ	A3

Allow one student to read the "treasure."

> The very first Hebrew word in Scripture is "b-re-SHEET" בְּרֵאשִׁית. (Genesis 1:1)
> It means "in the beginning" and includes the three new letters. "b-re-SHEET" comes from the Hebrew root meaning "head, beginning, first or front" and is also the root of the Hebrew word "rosh" (head). Just as the LORD created the heavens and the earth, He also promises that He "will make you the **head** [rosh] and not the tail." (Deuteronomy 28:13 NIV, emphasis added).

A4

Read Hebrew from right to left!   A5

Read the names of the letters on the next line, then, read the sounds of the letters:

שׁ בּ ת שׁ ת בּ שׁ ת בּ שׁ בּ ת ← A6

B - Vowels

Allow students to work as partners as much as possible. For example, partners can practice reading a line of letter combinations to each other before speaking out loud to the entire class.

Sound	Vowel	
"a" as in **a**ll	◌ַ	B2
"a" as in **a**ll	◌ָ	B3

◌ = any letter   B1

Say the letter sound first, then the vowel (hint: think "up, down"): בַּ = "b" + "a" = "ba"   B4

שַׁ תַּ בַּ שָׁ שַׁ בָּ תַּ שַׁ בַּ   B5

(hint: think "up, down, left"): תַּשׁ "t" + "a" + "sh" = "tash"   B6

Ask students to turn to the Lesson Fill-in Page.

daughter בַּת   תַת שַׁב בַּב שַׁת תַשׁ בַּשׁ בַּשׁ   B7

For English meaning see Lesson Fill-Ins

*Encourage students **not** to write the transliterations above the Hebrew!*

Lesson 1 ש ת ב | HWJ Teacher's Guide

*In Hebrew Sephardic pronunciation, <u>most</u> words are accented on the **last** syllable. B8

*Example with two letters and two vowels: בַּתָ = "ba-TA"

Sephardic Pronunciation is used in the middle East, Israel and Spain. Ashkenazi Pronunciation is used in Eastern Europe and America (accent on 1st syllable).

Read the following combinations 2 times:

בַּשָׁ תָּתְ תָּשׁ שַׁתּ בַּתָ   B9

*Example with three letters and two vowels: בַּתָשׁ = "ba-TASH" B10

<u>Sabbath</u> שַׁבָּת בָּתָשׁ תָּתָשׁ שָׁבַשׁ בָּתָשׁ   B11
See Lesson Fill-Ins

Word Meaning	Key Word	Root Meaning	Root	
Sabbath	שַׁבָּת	rest, stop	שׁ.ב.ת	C1

C - Roots

English also uses Roots – Example is "AUD" as in audition, audible, auditorium. All are related to <u>hearing</u>.

Most Hebrew words are built from three letters called a **ROOT**	C2
Middle and bottom dots and vowels are not written in roots	C3
Words from the same root share similar meanings	C4
Vowels, prefixes and suffixes change the meaning Example: שַׁבָּתוֹן (sha-ba-TON) means "sabbatical"	C5

Circle the Hebrew root for "rest/stop" in the following Scripture: C6
(Remember that there may be extra letters before or after the root.)

Ask if any student can read the scripture. If not, read it slowly first, then read it at full speed.

זָכוֹר אֶת־יוֹם הַשַּׁבָּת לְקַדְּשׁוֹ.

za-KHOR et-yom ha-sha-BAT l-kad-SHO

Remember the Sabbath day to keep it holy. (see Exodus 20:8)

שַׁבָּת

Exodus 31:13 tells us that keeping the Shabbat (Sabbath) on the seventh day is a sign of the covenant between Adonai (God) and those who love Him. The Shabbat is one of His "mo-a-DEEM" (appointed times). Just as He rested on the seventh day after creation, He has asked us to honor His commandment to take a day of rest. His blessings will follow!   C7

D - Writing

Write each letter or vowel three times in block or script then make a flashcard to help you:

**Script	Practice then make flashcards	Block	Letter	
כ		בּ	בּ	D1
e	*If a student already knows the Alef-Bet, encourage them to learn the script – this will help if they take a trip to Israel as many signs are in script. Also, it's helpful for writing Hebrew prayers.*	שׁ	שׁ	D2
ת		ת	ת	D3
		ָ		D4

Encourage the students to create their flashcards in class. It's easier if they cut the 3X5 cards in half and use a pen (not a marker as it will bleed.) Rubber bands will keep their pile of cards together.

**Normally, vowels and dots are not written in script.   D5

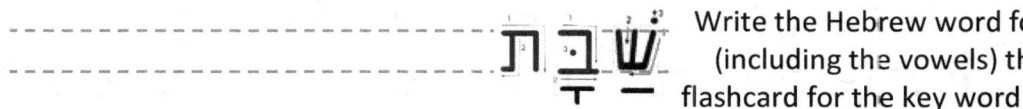 Write the Hebrew word for "Sabbath" (including the vowels) then make a flashcard for the key word *and* the root: D6

Remind students to create flashcards for all the letters, vowels, Roots and key words!.

Lesson 1 ב ת שׁ   HWJ Teacher's Guide

Name _____   Exercises Lesson 1

Read the following letter combinations two times: ⇐

1. בַּ שָׁ שֵׁת תַשׁ בַּת תָת בַּתְשׁ שַׁבָּת

Homework suggestions:

Practice writing each letter and vowel combination ten times in block or script:

2. בְּ ....

3. שׁ ....

4. ת ....

1. Have partners check each other's homework at the beginning of the next class.

2. Students can email or text photos of their homework to teacher.

Circle the letters that make the same sound as the letters on the far right:

5. שֵׁת ⇐ בַּת תַשׁ שֵׁת בָּשׁ תַת (שֵׁת) שַׁב
6. בַּת ⇐ (בַּת) תַשׁ שֵׁת בָּשׁ תַת שָׁת שַׁב (בַּת)
7. תָת ⇐ בַּת (תָת) שָׁת בָּשׁ שַׁב בָּת (תָת)
8. בַּבּ ⇐ בַּת שָׁת תַת בַּבּ תַת שֵׁת שַׁב (בַּבּ)

3. Teachers, be sure to check that vowels are included and that students have completed their practice letters.

9. Write the Hebrew word for "Sabbath" 3 times:
....
....

10. In **Sephardic** Hebrew, which syllable usually receives the accent? Circle the correct answer:

First   Middle   Second-to-Last   (Last)

11. Write Hebrew letters and vowels that have the same sound as the following English words:

שֹׁת שֹׁת shot   בָּת בָּת bought   תָת תָת taught

This is a challenge for new students. Point out the example for "taught" BEFORE the students attempt the homework.

12. Make your own flashcards by writing each new letter and vowel on one side of a notecard and its sound on the other side. Then practice until they are memorized.

Exercises Lesson 1

13. What is the meaning of the Hebrew **ROOT** ש.ב.ת ?

   rest/stop

14. Circle the word for "Sabbath" in the following Scripture - Exodus 20:8:

   זָכוֹר אֶת־יוֹם הַ(שַּׁבָּת) לְקַדְּשׁוֹ.

15. Write the English translation of Exodus 20:8:

   Remember the Sabbath day to keep it holy.   Exodus 20:8

16. Circle the roots for "rest/stop" in Isaiah 58:13-14:

אִם־תָּשִׁיב מִ(שַּׁבָּת) רַגְלֶךָ עֲשׂוֹת חֲפָצֶיךָ בְּיוֹם קָדְשִׁי וְקָרָאתָ לַ(שַּׁבָּת) עֹנֶג לִקְדוֹשׁ יְהוָה מְכֻבָּד וְכִבַּדְתּוֹ מֵעֲשׂוֹת דְּרָכֶיךָ מִמְּצוֹא חֶפְצְךָ וְדַבֵּר דָּבָר:

אָז תִּתְעַנַּג עַל־יְהוָה וְהִרְכַּבְתִּיךָ עַל־בָּמוֹתֵי /עַל־בָּמֳתֵי/ אָרֶץ וְהַאֲכַלְתִּיךָ נַחֲלַת יַעֲקֹב אָבִיךָ כִּי פִּי יְהוָה דִּבֵּר:

17. *In your own words, (in English) summarize Isaiah 58:13-14:*

At beginning of next lesson, ask 1 or 2 students to share their summary.

HWJ Teacher's Guide | Lesson 2 ל מ ם

Lesson 2   ל מ ם

Be sure to review the previous phrases, letters, vowels, key words, and roots at the start of each lesson.

Israeli Phrases
Nice to meet you!   na-EEM m-OD!
See you later!   l-heet-ra-OT!

Start from the back! Use the "Long Word" suggestion in the Teacher Introduction.

A - Letters

Sound	Name	Letter	
"l" as in light	**LA**-med	ל	A1
"m" as in molehill	Mem	מ	A2
"m" as in molehill	Mem so-FEET* (used at the end of a word)	ם	A3

so-FEET = "Final"- Mem is one of five Hebrew letters that change their form at the end of a word.   A4

The five so-FEET letters are Mem ם Nun ן Kaf ך Pay ף and TSA-dee ץ.

Read each line two times:

שָׁ לְ תָ מַ בְּ תַם מֶם תֵל מַב   A5

בַּם לָם תַם מָלַם מַתָשׁ שַׁבָּת שָׁם   ___there___   A6

*During **Chanukah**, the Feast of Dedication, the traditional **dreidel** (spinning top) game is played. In America, the four Hebrew letters on the dreidel stand for the words "A Great Miracle Happened THERE." שׁ stands for "there" – from the word שָׁם (sham). But, in Israel, this letter changes to a פ. Then, they stand for "A Great Miracle happened HERE!" (Po פֹּה)*   A7

Bring a dreidel to show the class.

B - Vowels

Ask students to point "over" their head to remember the "o" sound.

Sound	Vowel	
"o" as in "over" (dot is **O**VER the letter)	וֹ	B1
	ֹ	B2

Read each line two times:

שׁוֹ מוֹ ל שׁ תֹ לֹם בּוֹם שֹׁת תּוֹת   B3

שֹׁם מוֹת תּוֹשׁ שְׁמוֹ תּוֹלָם שָׁלוֹם   ___peace/hello /goodbye___   B4

Lesson 2   ל מ ם   HWJ Teacher's Guide

Write each letter or vowel three times in block or script then *make a flashcard* to help you study:

C - Writing

Again, stress the importance of flashcards and practicing daily.

Script	Practice then make a flashcard	Block	Letter	
ℓ		ל	ל	C1
N		מ	מ	C2
ρ		ם	ם	C3
ו		וֹ	וֹ	C4

D - Root

Word Meaning	Key Word	Root Meaning	Root	
peace, hello, goodbye	שָׁלוֹם	completion, wholeness	ש.ל.ם	D1
At times, extra letters may be added between root letters. For instance, in שָׁלוֹם, the וֹ is added				D2

"Jerusalem" (y-roo-sha-**LAI**-yeem in Hebrew) *comes from the root* ש.ל.ם
  y-roo= they will see
  sha-lem = peace, wholeness, completion, and perfection
  sha-**LAI**-yeem= "**LAI**-yeem" ending means <u>double</u> shalom!   D3

Circle the words for "peace" in the following scripture:

יֵצֶר סָמוּךְ תִּצֹּר שָׁלוֹם שָׁלוֹם   D4

YE-tser sa-**MOOKH** tee-**TSOR** sha-**LOM** sha-**LOM**

You keep in perfect peace one whose mind is stayed on You. (Isaiah 26:3)

Write the Key Word (include the vowels) then make a flashcard for the key word *and* the root:

שָׁלוֹם   D5

You can now read the following beloved Sabbath greeting: שַׁבָּת שָׁלוֹם!   D6

> **Paleo-Hebrew**
> The letters we are studying today have evolved over the centuries. Originally, the **Paleo-Hebrew** letters represented pictures with special meanings.
> (For more study, search online for Ancient Hebrew, Picto-Hebrew or Paleo Hebrew)

D7

"Shalom" study by Dr. I Suuquina:				
ם	ו	ל	שׁ	Modern Letter
∿	Y	∫	ш	Ancient Letter
water	nail	staff	teeth	Letter Meaning
chaos	attach	authority	destroy	Deeper Meaning

D8

Shalom: **Destroying** the **authority attached** to **chaos**.

For more resources by Dr. I. Suuquina, check out their website:
http://www.indigenousmessengers.com

Lesson 2   ל מ ם   *HWJ Teacher's Guide*

Slap Game: *If you are studying in a group, one person reads a combination, then, two other people try to be the first to **slap** that combination (or say the square number.) After reading all the combinations, rotate so there is a new reader. If you are studying by yourself, read each combination two times.*

If you are using the Teacher PPTs, give fly swatters to two students to "slap" the right answer on the screen.

4	3	2	1
מֶלֶשׁ	שָׁם	בַּשׁ	מוֹת
8	**7**	**6**	**5**
לֹם	תַּתְ	לָתָשׁ	תוֹם
12	**11**	**10**	**9**
לוֹמֶת	מָלֹת	שָׁלוֹם	בּוֹת
16	**15**	**14**	**13**
לָלֹת	שַׁבָּת	שׁוֹת	מוֹל

HWJ Teacher's Guide　　　　　　　　　　　　　　　　　　　　　　　Lesson 2　ל מ ם

Name _____　Exercises Lesson 2

1. Read the following letter combinations three times:

שָׁלוֹם　תּוֹלָם　שְׁמוֹ　שַׁבָּת　שָׁם　תָּל　מוֹת　לָת

Practice writing each letter and vowel combination ten times in block or script:

2. לָ
3. מֲ
4. ם
5. וֹ

24　Write 2 *different* Hebrew combinations that sound like each English word (include vowels):
(Remember to use the right form of Mem)

6. Tom　תָּם　תָּם
7. mole　מוֹל　מוֹל
8. ball　בָּל　בָּל

9. Mom　מֶם　מָם
10. mall　מָל　מָל
11. boat　בּוֹת　בָּת

12. Circle the words for "peace" in Isaiah 26:3:

יֵצֶר סָמוּךְ תִּצֹּר ⟨שָׁלוֹם⟩ ⟨שָׁלוֹם⟩ כִּי בְךָ בָּטוּחַ׃

13. Write the English meaning of Isaiah 26:3:

You keep in perfect peace one whose mind is stayed on You.

14. Write the Hebrew words for "Sabbath peace" two times (include vowels):

שַׁבָּת שָׁלוֹם　　　　　שַׁבָּת שָׁלוֹם

Exercises Lesson 2

15. What is the meaning of the Hebrew root ש.ל.ם ?

    _____completion/wholeness_____

Circle the root letters ש.ל.ם in the following words:

16. to pay/complete a transaction (l-sha-LEM)

17. Solomon/man of peace (**SHLO**-mo)

18. Jerusalem/city of peace (y-roo-sha-**LAI**-yeem)

19. complete/perfect (moo-SHLAM)

20. complete healing (r-foo-AH shle-MA)

21. Circle the words for "peace" (eight times) in this traditional Hebrew prayer, Oseh Shalom:

עוֹשֶׂה שָׁלוֹם בִּמְרוֹמָיו הוּא יַעֲשֶׂה שָׁלוֹם עָלֵינוּ
וְעַל כָּל יִשְׂרָאֵל, וְאִמְרוּ, וְאִמְרוּ: אָמֵן
יַעֲשֶׂה שָׁלוֹם יַעֲשֶׂה שָׁלוֹם עָלֵינוּ וְעַל כָּל יִשְׂרָאֵל
יַעֲשֶׂה שָׁלוֹם יַעֲשֶׂה שָׁלוֹם עָלֵינוּ וְעַל כָּל יִשְׂרָאֵל

22. Look up this Hebrew prayer (Oseh Shalom) on the internet and write the English translation:

He who makes peace in His high places, may He bring peace upon us and upon all Israel and say Amen. May He bring peace, may He bring peace, peace upon us and on all of Israel. May He bring peace, may He bring peace, peace upon us and on all of Israel.

23. By yourself or with a partner, use your flashcards to practice the sounds of the letters and vowels in Lessons 1 and 2. Make sure that you know them before starting Lesson 3!

HWJ Teacher's Guide   Lesson 3   ר י ה

Lesson 3   ר י ה

Don't forget to review!

Ask students to stand up as you teach a motion for each greeting: IE. Wake-up stretch for BO-ker tov, 2 hands together under one cheek for LAI-la tov, hands forward and going down for E-rev tov and point forward for sha-VOO-a tov.

Israeli Greetings

BO-ker tov   **E**-rev tov   **LAI**-la tov   sha-**VOO**-a tov
(good morning)   (good evening)   (good night)   (good week)

A - Letters

Sound	Name	Letter	
"**r**" as in **r**est (This is a "guttural" sound made in the back of the throat)	Raysh	ר	A1
"**y**" as in **y**es	Yud/Yod	י	A2
"**h**" as in **h**oly or **silent** at the end of a word (Hay has a **h**ole!)	Hay	ה	A3

Raysh is the first guttural letter. Have students try to say the Raysh in the back of the throat. Let them know if it is hard, make the normal "r" sound.

> The open space in the ה is like a door - no matter how far we've strayed, Adonai always leaves a way, a space, an opening for turning back to Him!   A4

Read each line two times and translate the words on the second line:

רַ   ר׳   הָ   הוּ   יָר   רָה   יה   שָׁר   תּוֹר   יָר   A5

תּוֹרָה   יוֹם   מוֹרָה   יָהּ   מָה   הַר   A6
instruction   day   teacher (f)   LORD   what   mountain   A7

The dot inside the ה does not change the letter sound.   A8
Only three Hebrew letters change their sound when a dot is added inside: פ כ ב
(With the dot, the letter has a harder sound)
To remember the three letters, think of the sounds in "backpack:"
B.K.P.K.

B.K.P.K letters and sounds:

soft		hard	
"v"	ב	"b"	בּ
"kh"	כ	"k"	כּ
"f"	פ	"p"	פּ

27

Lesson 3 ה ר י   HWJ Teacher's Guide

B - Roots

Word Meaning	Key Word	Root Meaning	Root	
Instruction, teaching, law, first five books of the Bible	תּוֹרָה	hit the mark	י.ר.ה.	B1
	In some words, one or more of the root letters drop. For instance, in תּוֹרָה, the י drops			B2

Circle the Hebrew word for "instruction" (first and last root letters drop!):

שָׁלוֹם רָב לְאֹהֲבֵי תוֹרָתֶךָ   B3

sha-LOM rav l-o-ha-VAY to-ra-TE-kha

Great peace have those who love Your instruction.   Psalm 119:165

> *Jewish scholars use a style of study called a **MIDRASH** - an intense, sometimes loud and lively group study of the Torah. Jews believe that "Torah instruction and knowledge is not gained except in the company of others." What a blessing that we also have the **ROO**-akh ha-**KO**-desh (Holy Spirit) to teach us!*   B4

C - Writing

Script	Practice then make flashcards	Block	Letter	
ר		ר	ר	C1
י		י	י	C2
ה		ה	ה	C3

Write the key word meaning "instruction" (include the vowels) then make a flashcard for the key word *and* the root:

תּוֹרָה   C4

D - Vowels

Sound	Vowel	
"e" as in egg (as in two eggs in a basket)	ֶ	D1
"e" as in egg (as in three eggs in a basket)	ֱ	D2
"e" as in egg (as in five eggs in a basket)	ֵ	D3

Make flashcards for the vowels above: D4

Read the combinations two times: D5

שֵׁם שֶׁל הֵם בֵּל יֵל רֵם הֵר
name ___ ___ ___ ___ ___ ___ ___

When the ֶ appears twice (side-by-side) the first one is accented as in **SHE**-mesh שֶׁמֶשׁ D6

Students may be familiar with other words using this rule:
ME-lekh – king
LE-khem – bread
E-rev - evening

שֶׁמֶשׁ מֹשֶׁה מוֹרֶה הַשֵּׁם D7
sun   Moses   teacher (m)   the name D8

Sometimes, two letters share the same dot: מֹשֶׁה D9

E - Prefix הַ

Note that a dot (dagesh) is sometimes added to the letter following the הַ.

Use the prefix הַ to add "the" before a Hebrew word:
Note: sometimes a dot is added in the letter following the הַ. E1

the = הַ   the name = הַשֵּׁם

Read each word then write the English translation of the following: E2

הַתּוֹרָה   הַשַׁבָּת   הַשָׁלוֹם
the instruction   the Sabbath   the peace

> "The ability of the הַ to add individuality and character to a word is indicative of what also happens to any person when the Holy Spirit is breathed into their lives…they progress from being just "a" person to being "the" person God has made in His own image."
> **In His Own Words** by L. Grant Luton p.63

E3

Lesson 3 - **Board Game**: *Each player or team needs a different marker. With a partner or by yourself, roll a die and move forward the number on the die. Each time you land on a word, read it and try to translate:*

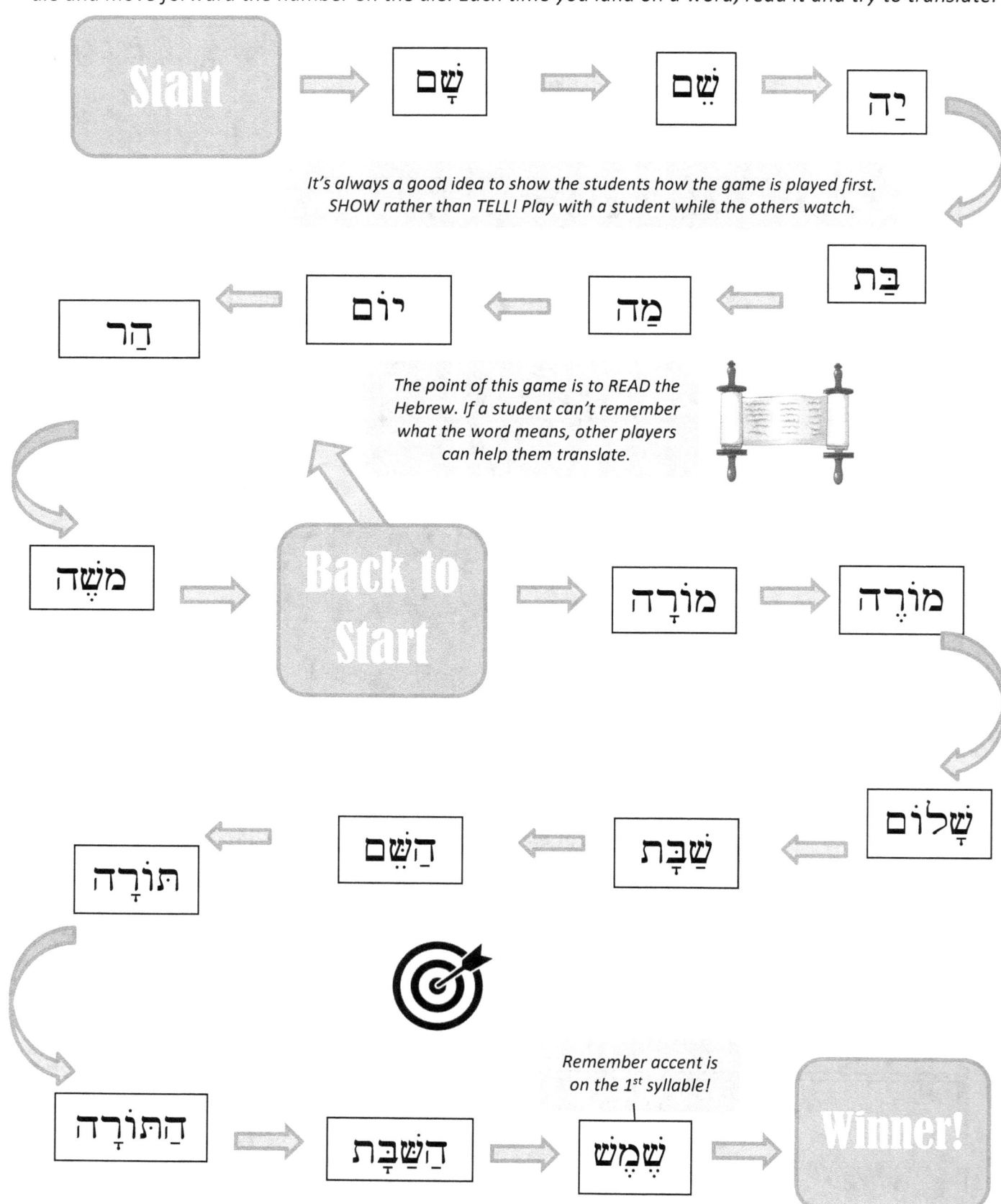

HWJ Teacher's Guide   Lesson 3   ר ה י

Exercises Lesson 3   שֵׁם _____

Read aloud two times and translate these Hebrew words:

1. מֹשֶׁה שֶׁמֶשׁ דַּר הַשֵּׁם בַּת תּוֹרָה שָׁלוֹם שַׁבָּת

Using numbers, match the Hebrew phrases to their meaning:

9 Good evening	**BO**-ker tov .6	**5** My name is …	l-heet-ra-OT .2
7 Good week	sha-**VOO**-a tov .7	**4** Hello	na-EEM m-OD .3
6 Good morning	**LAI**-la tov .8	**2** See you later!	שָׁלוֹם .4
8 Good night	**E**-rev tov .9	**3** Nice to meet you	sh-mee .5

Practice writing each combination 10 times in block or script:

10. רְ

11. הַ

12. רֱ

Circle the Hebrew letters that sound like the English words:

13. hall → הֶל ⟨הַל⟩ ⟨הָל⟩ תַל הוֹל הֵל
14. bet → בֵּת ⟨בֶּת⟩ בַּת ⟨בֵּת⟩ בֶּה בּוֹה בֶּת בַּת
15. yet → יוֹת ⟨יֶת⟩ ⟨יֵת⟩ יִת רֵת יַת יָה
16. home → הֶם ⟨הֹם⟩ תֹם הֹם ⟨הוֹם⟩

17. Write the following words in Hebrew (include vowels):

the name	Sabbath	peace	instruction
הַשֵּׁם	שַׁבָּת	שָׁלוֹם	תּוֹרָה

Lesson 3   ר י ה   HWJ Teacher's Guide

Exercises Lesson 3

18. Circle the word for "instruction" in the Hebrew Scripture Jeremiah 31:32(33):

נָתַתִּי אֶת־(תּוֹרָתִי) בְּקִרְבָּם וְעַל־לִבָּם אֶכְתֲבֶנָּה

19. Fill in the missing English word:

"I will put My __Torah/instruction__ within them and write it on their heart" Jeremiah 31:32(33)

20. Write the meaning of the Hebrew ROOT י.ר.ה ?

__hit the mark__

Write the English names of the five books of the תּוֹרָה below (**Note**: They are not in order!):
You may want to search the internet for "Hebrew names of the books of the Bible"

	English Name	Meaning of the Hebrew Name	Transliteration	Hebrew Name
21.	Numbers	In the desert/wilderness	ba-**MEED**-bar	בְּמִדְבַּר
22.	Leviticus	And He called	va-**YEE**-kra	וַיִּקְרָא
23.	Genesis	In the beginning	b-re-**SHEET**	בְּרֵאשִׁית
24.	Exodus	Names	sh-**MOT**	שְׁמוֹת
25.	Deuteronomy	Words/Things	d-va-**REEM**	דְּבָרִים

Being called up to recite the Torah blessing during a service is considered a great honor!
In Hebrew, this is called making "Aliyah" = meaning "to go up".

26. Circle the words for "instruction" in this Hebrew prayer that is chanted before reading the Torah:

בָּרוּךְ אַתָּה יְהוָה אֱלֹהֵינוּ מֶלֶךְ הָעוֹלָם אֲשֶׁר בָּחַר בָּנוּ מִכָּל הָעַמִּים
וְנָתַן לָנוּ אֶת (תּוֹרָתוֹ). בָּרוּךְ אַתָּה יְהוָה נוֹתֵן הַ(תּוֹרָה).

Blessed are You, LORD our God, King of the universe, who has chosen us from among all the nations and given us His Torah. Blessed are You LORD, giver of the Torah.

Lesson 4 א ע ן נ

> **Israeli Greetings**
> How's it going?   ma neesh-MA?
> Good, thanks!   tov, to-DA!

A - Letters

Sound	Name	Letter	
"n" as in name	Nun	נ	A1
"n" as in name	Nun so-FEET (Final Nun)	ן	A2
Silent (takes the vowel sound)	**AY**-in	ע	A3
Silent (takes the vowel sound)	**A**-lef	א	A4

> א is the first letter of the Hebrew Alef-Bet so it has a number value of "one." (e-KHAD)
> א represents the Holy "One" of Israel and is also the first letter in these names of God:
> e-lo-HEEM אֱלֹהִים (God) and a-do-NAI אֲדוֹנָי (God/my Master)

A5

Read each line twice and translate the words on the second line:

יָן מֶן דֶן נַת נֹ אֶל נוּ אוּ עַ א   A6

אָמֵן אַבָּא בֵּן אוֹר אַתָּה עַם אֵל   A7
amen/so be it · Daddy · son · light · you (ms) · people · God/god   A8

B - Writing

Script	Practice then make flashcards	Block	Letter	
		נ	נ	B1
		ן	ן	B2
		ע	ע	B3
		א	א	B4

Lesson 4 נ ע | א　　　　　　　　　　　　　　　　　　　　　　HWJ Teacher's Guide

C - Vowels

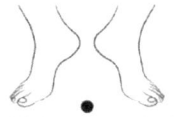

Sound	Vowel	
"ee" as in "f<u>ee</u>t" The vowel is under the letter's feet!	�ִ	C1
"ee" as in "f<u>ee</u>t" (The Yood in a vowel has the "ee" sound)	יִ	C2

The "ee" vowel is one of the hardest for new students! Have students stand up pointing above head for "o" sound and pointing at their feet for "ee" sound.

Make flashcards for the vowels above:　C3

Read this line 2 times:

C4　הִ　עִי　תְא　לִים　יָן　בִּין　אֲנִי ___I___

Silent or short "uh" as in <u>u</u>pon (one dot is <u>u</u>pon the other!)	Sh-va	ְ	C5
Sh-va Examples			
At the **beginning of a word**, the short "uh" sound		שְׁמַע	C6
In the **middle of a word**, usually stops a syllable and is silent (If there are two Sh-vas side by side, the first is silent, the second has the short "uh" sound)		לְהִתְרָאוֹת *Vertical line = syllable break.*	C7
At the **end of a word**: always silent		אַתְּ	C8

Throughout class, use syllable lines to help students pronounce words correctly (see Lesson 10.)

Make a flashcard for the sh-va:　C9

Read this line two times:

C10　עִית　תְּשׁ　נֵר　לֶם　מְא　נֶשׁ　אַתְּ　you (fs)

Read this line two times then translate:

C11　לְהִתְרָאוֹת　מְנוֹרָה　שְׁלֹמֹה　בְּרִית

C12　see you later　candlestick/lamp　Solomon　covenant

The בְּרִית מִילָה "covenant of circumcision" takes place on the eighth day of a Jewish boy's life when he is also given his name! (see Leviticus 12:3) An Israeli tradition is to take the baby's foreskin, bury it in the yard and plant a new tree right above, signifying new life!　C13

HWJ Teacher's Guide   Lesson 4   א ו ע נ

Read this line two times then translate:

שְׁמַע	הַבָּא	אֱלֹהִים	C14
hear/listen	the one who comes	God	C15

D - Root

Word Meaning	Key Word	Root Meaning	Root	
hear! listen!	שְׁמַע	hear and obey	שׁ.מ.ע	D1

If any of the students know the Sh'ma prayer, ask them to say or sing it by themselves or as a class. Jews traditionally stand and face the East (toward Jerusalem) while reciting it.

Circle the word for "hear" in Deuteronomy 6:4:

שְׁמַע יִשְׂרָאֵל יְהוָה אֱלֹהֵינוּ יְהוָה אֶחָד׃   D2

sh-MA yees-ra-EL a-do-NAI e-lo-HAY-noo a-do-NAI e-KHAD

Hear (O) Israel, The LORD our God, the LORD is one.

Note: יְהוָה means "the LORD" and can be pronounced "a-do-NAI."

If you have a mezuzah, bring it to show your class.

The שְׁמַע Sh'ma (Deuteronomy 6:4), is the most beloved prayer in Judaism, recited three times a day by religiously observant Jews. It is found in the mezuzah (prayer box on the doorposts) along with these Scriptures: Deuteronomy 5:5-9 and 11:13-21 Inside the Phylacteries (leather prayer boxes wrapped around the arm and forehead) are these scriptures: Deuteronomy 6:4-9, 11:13-21, Exodus 13:1-10, 11-16.	D3

Write the Hebrew word for "hear" and make a flashcard for the key word *and* the root (Don't forget the vowels!):   D4

35

Tic Tac Toe

Before starting the game, make ten game pieces – five of one color and five of another. Each player picks a color. To play the game, one player puts a piece down on a square and must read and translate the word. Then the opponent plays. The object is to be the first to have three pieces of their color in a row (vertical, horizontal or diagonal).

*If you have foreign students, they may not have played Tic Tac Toe before.
If so, play one game with a student and have all the students watch.*

אַבָּא	תּוֹרָה	שָׁלוֹם
הַבָּא	שְׁמַע	אֱלֹהִים
בְּרִית	שַׁבָּת	הַשֵּׁם

Exercises Lesson 4

שֵׁם _____

Read and translate these words:

1. אֵל עַם אוֹר אַבָּא אָמֵן שַׁבָּת תּוֹרָה שְׁמַע שָׁלוֹם

Using numbers, match the Hebrew words to their meaning:

_7_ good morning	tov to-DA .6	_5_ hear	אַתָּה .2
_9_ how are you	**BO**-ker tov .7	_4_ Dad	בֵּן .3
_6_ good, thanks	**LAI**-la tov .8	_3_ son	אַבָּא .4
_8_ good night	ma neesh-MA .9	_2_ you (masc)	שְׁמַע .5

Translate the English words into Hebrew letters in the puzzle below – DON'T USE VOWELS!

*Before students complete this puzzle, remind them **not** to use vowels.*

.10 amen
.11 peace
.12 hear
.13 instruction

Notice the small letters (a,b,c,d) in the squares of the puzzle above.
Copy the Hebrew letter from those squares to the line below:

.14 a שׁ ___ b ל ___ c מ ___ d ה

.15 What is the English name for the king in line 14? ____Solomon____

Write the correct form of the Nun in the following words from the lesson then translate to English:

.16 אָמֵן /amen/so be it   אֲנִי I   מְנוֹרָה lamp/candlestick

.17 Practice writing each new combination four times:

| נְ | אָן | עִר |

Exercises Lesson 4

18. Write the English translation of the Sh'ma: (Deuteronomy 6:4)

שְׁמַע יִשְׂרָאֵל יְהוָה אֱלֹהֵינוּ יְהוָה אֶחָד׃	Hebrew
Hear, Israel! The LORD our God the LORD is one.	English

19. What is the meaning of the Hebrew root שׁ.מ.ע ?

hear/obey

Most English Bibles break **Psalm 119** into sections.
Open a bible that does this and answer the following questions:

20. Which English translation did you use? _____
21. How many sections are in Psalm 119? __22__
22. How many verses are in each section? __8__
23. How are the sections named? __Alef-Bet__
24. What is the name of the first section? __Alef__
25. What is the name of the last section? __Tav__
26. Do you have a favorite verse from Psalm 119? If so, which verse? _____

After students finish this homework, ask if 1 or 2 students would like to share their favorite verse from Psalm 119 and why it is their favorite.

Write the English meaning for the following words from the lesson which all start with א.

27. אַבָּא __Dad/Daddy__
28. אֱלֹהִים __God__
29. אֶחָד __one__ (Hint – from the Sh'ma)

Lesson 5   כ ך ח

Spend some time practicing the "kh" sound. Ask students to feel their throats as they pronounce the sound.

Israeli Greetings
How's it going?   ma neesh-MA?
OK/fine   b-**SE**-der

Practice all previous phrases. Use a soft toy for students to toss (Ex. Student 1 says "shalom, sh'mee Don" then tosses to another student who answers.)

A - Letters

Sound	Name	Letter	
"kh" as in Ba**ch** (This is a "guttural" sound made in the back of the throat)	Kaf (without a dot) (BKPK letter - no dot softens the sound)	כ	A1
	Kaf so-FEET* (Final Kaf)	ך	A2
	Khet	ח	A3

*Kaf so-FEET has two forms: ךְ "kh" or ךָ "khah"   A4

ח represents "life" (khai-YEEM) חַיִּים. It is common for Jewish women to wear a חַי (khai - "live") necklace to represent the incredible importance of *life* to the Jewish people. From the Passover story in Exodus 12:22-23, the doorposts that the angel of death passed over (providing life) were in the shape of a ח.	A5

Name of a Torah portion! → לֵךְ לְךָ לֶךְ

Read the following line two times:
כַ ח כוֹ כֹת חֵ חֶן אַךְ   A6

Read and then translate:
king מֶלֶךְ   _bread_ לֶחֶם   _Rachel_ רָחֵל   A7

Remember accent is on the first syllable!

B - Writing

Script	Practice then make flashcards	Block	Letter	
ͻ		ב	כ	B1
ρ		ך	ך	B2
π		ח	ח	B3

C – Look-Alike Letters

כָ נָ	Kaf is wider	C4	הֵ חֵ	Hay has a hole	C1
רֵ	Raysh is shorter	C5	בֵ כֵ	Bet has a bottom bar. Both can have dots!	C2
ךָ	Kaf SoFEET is longer	C6	תֵ חֵ	Tav has a toe!	C3

Ask each student to read one look alike pair.   Read the following line two times:

C7   בְּח בְּה לת לח כן בן כות נות לֵךְ לְךָ

D - Vowels

This is the last of the single-dot vowels. Ask students to stand up and point to the "o" sound (above head), the "ee" sound (under the feet) and the "oo" sound (point to stomach.)

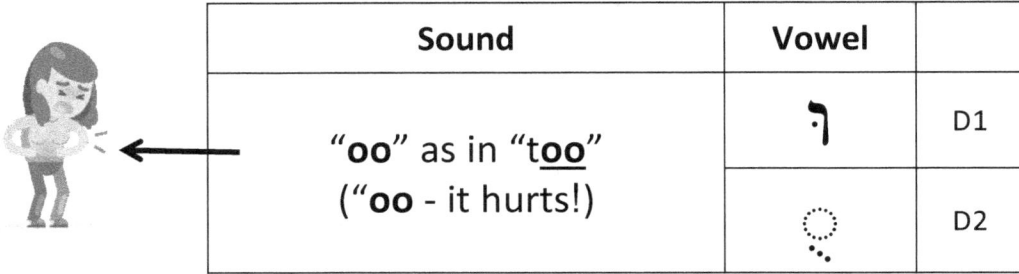

Sound	Vowel	
"**oo**" as in "t**oo**" ("**oo** - it hurts!")	וּ	D1
	ֻ	D2

Make flashcards for the vowels above: D3

Read the following line two times:

D4   כוּ רוּ מֻ נֻם בֻּ לוּד חוּשִׁי רָעֻךָ

Read the following line two times, then translate the words:

D5   רוּת הַלְלוּיָהּ אֱמוּנָה יְשׁוּעָה בָּרוּךְ

D6   Ruth   hallelujah   faith   salvation   blessed

E - Root

Word Meaning	Key Word	Root Meaning	Root
blessed	בָּרוּךְ	bless, kneel	ב.ר.ך

E1

E2 בְּרָכָה Blessing or Benediction

E3 בֶּרֶךְ Knee (bow the knee)

E4 בָּרוּךְ הַבָּא Blessed is the comer - Welcome! (to one person)
Used to greet a new baby

E5 בְּרוּכִים הַבָּאִים Blessed are the comers - Welcome! (to a group)
Wedding greeting for a new couple

*b-roo-KHEEM ha-ba-EEM
Bleesed are the comers –
"Welcome" to a group.*

If you see this sign, you are on Hwy 1 driving into Jerusalem. What does the sign say?

E6

Write the Hebrew word for "blessed" then make a flashcard for the key word *and* the root:

E7

בָּרוּךְ הַבָּא בְּשֵׁם יְהוָה.

ba-ROOKH ha-BA b-SHEM a-do-NAI

Blessed is the one who comes in the name of the LORD. Psalm 118:26

E8

יְהוָה means "the LORD" and can be pronounced "a-do-NAI."

E9

בָּרוּךְ אַתָּה יהוה...

"Blessed are you, Adonai…" These beloved words begin many Jewish prayers,
a testimony to the reverence and devotion belonging to Adonai alone.
Many of these prayers are included in Jewish holidays (mo-a-DEEM) - appointments
with God. Every Friday evening at sundown, Jewish homes around the world celebrate
the beginning of Shabbat by reciting these prayers: Lighting the Shabbat Candles,
Blessing the Bread and Blessing the Wine. On the following pages,
you can practice these prayers and experience your own Shabbat celebration.

E10

Shabbat Handout

Encourage students to read all of the prayers on the following 2 pages– the transliterations are included because not all of the letters have been taught. By the end of the book, students should be able to read all the Hebrew!

In the Homework for this lesson, students are asked to celebrate Shabbat using these prayers. Remind them that these pages are only a guide – a springboard to make Shabbat their own special celebration.

Shabbat שַׁבָּת

Exodus 20:8-11 *"Remember Yom Shabbat [day of Shabbat] to keep it holy. You are to work six days, and do all your work, but the seventh day is a Shabbat to Adonai your God. In it you shall not do any work... For in six days Adonai made heaven and earth, the sea, and all that is in them, and rested on the seventh day. Thus Adonai blessed Yom Shabbat, and made it holy."*

Isaiah 58:13-14 *"If you turn back your foot from Shabbat, from doing your pleasure on My holy day, and call Shabbat a delight, the holy day of Adonai honorable, if you honor it, not going your own ways, not seeking your own pleasure, nor speaking your usual speech, then You will delight yourself in Adonai, and I will let you ride over the heights of the earth. I will feed you with the heritage of your father Jacob."*

Candle Lighting Prayer
(new prayer from Exodus 20:8)

בָּרוּךְ אַתָּה יְהוָה אֱלֹהֵינוּ מֶלֶךְ הָעוֹלָם
אֲשֶׁר צִוָּנוּ לְכַבֵּד אֶת הַשַּׁבָּת וּלְקַדְּשָׁהּ. אָמֵן

ba-ROOKH a-TA a-do-NAI, e-lo-**HAY**-noo **ME**-lekh ha-o-LAM,
a-SHER tsee-**VA**-noo l-kha-BED et ha-sha-BAT ool-kad-SHA. *a-MEN*

*We praise You, Adonai our God, King of the universe,
who has commanded us to honor the Sabbath and to keep it holy. Amen*

HaMotsee (Who Brings Forth) - Blessing over the Bread

בָּרוּךְ אַתָּה יְהוָה אֱלֹהֵינוּ מֶלֶךְ הָעוֹלָם הַמּוֹצִיא לֶחֶם מִן הָאָרֶץ. אָמֵן

ba-ROOKH a-TA a-do-NAI, e-lo-**HAY**-noo **ME**-lekh ha-o-LAM, ha-**MO**-tsee **LE**-khem meen ha-**A**-rets. *a-MEN*
Blessed are You, Adonai our God, Ruler of the universe, who brings forth bread from the earth. Amen

Kiddush (Sanctification) - Blessing over the Wine

בָּרוּךְ אַתָּה יְהוָה אֱלֹהֵינוּ מֶלֶךְ הָעוֹלָם בּוֹרֵא פְּרִי הַגָּפֶן. אָמֵן.

ba-ROOKH a-TA a-do-NAI, e-lo-**HAY**-noo **ME**-lekh ha-o-LAM, bo-RE p-REE ha-**GA**-fen. *a-MEN*
Blessed are you, Adonai, our God, Ruler of the universe, creator of the fruit of the vine. Amen

Sh'ma

שְׁמַע יִשְׂרָאֵל יְהוָה אֱלֹהֵינוּ יְהוָה אֶחָד:
בָּרוּךְ שֵׁם כְּבוֹד מַלְכוּתוֹ לְעוֹלָם וָעֶד:

sh-MA yees-ra-EL a-do-NAI e-lo-**HAY**-noo a-do-NAI e-KHAD:
ba-ROOKH shem k-VOD mal-**KHOO**-to l-o-LAM va-ED.

*Hear (O) Israel, The LORD our God, the LORD is one.
Blessed is the name of His glorious kingdom for ever and ever.*

Family Blessings

For Sons:

May Adonai inspire you to love in the tradition of Abraham, Isaac and Jacob.
May you grow closer to Adonai, our LORD, in strength and dignity and shine His light to those around you!

For Daughters:

May Adonai inspire you to love in the tradition of Sarah and Rebekah, Rachel and Leah.
May you grow in the love of Adonai, our King, and be a light to the world!

Blessing the Parents: (by the children)

May God bless your love for one another and for us!

For the Wife (from Proverbs 31):

A woman of valor – who can find? She is to be valued above rubies. Her husband trusts in her, and so he lacks nothing. She does him good, never harm, all the days of her life. She reached out to those in need, and extends her hands to the poor. She is clothed in strength and dignity and she faces the future cheerfully. She speaks with wisdom: the law of kindness is on her lips. She shines with the love of Adonai to her family and in her community. Her children rise up and bless her; her husband sings her praises.

For the Husband (from Psalm 112):

Blessed is the man who fears and glorifies Adonai, who greatly delights in Adonai's commandments. The generation of the upright will be blessed. His household prospers, and his righteousness endures forever. Light shines in the darkness for the upright. For the one who is gracious, compassionate and just. He is not afraid of evil tidings; his mind is firm; trusting in Adonai. His heart is steady, he will not be afraid. He gives freely to the poor. His righteousness endures forever; his life is exalted in honor.

The Aaronic Blessing:

יְבָרֶכְךָ יְהוָה וְיִשְׁמְרֶךָ: יָאֵר יְהוָה פָּנָיו אֵלֶיךָ וִיחֻנֶּךָ:
יִשָּׂא יְהוָה פָּנָיו אֵלֶיךָ וְיָשֵׂם לְךָ שָׁלוֹם:

y-va-**RE**-kh-kha a-do-NAI v-yeesh-m-**RE**-kha; ya-ER a-do-NAI pa-NAV e-**LE**-kha vee-khoo-**NE**-kha;
yee-SA a-do-NAI pa-NAV e-**LE**-kha v-ya-SEM l-KHA sha-LOM

*"Adonai bless you and keep you! Adonai make His face to shine on you and be gracious to you!
Adonai turn his face to you and grant you shalom. Numbers 6:24-26*

Shabbat Shalom! שַׁבָּת שָׁלוֹם!

HWJ Teacher's Guide   Lesson 5 כ ך ח

Exercises Lesson 5
_____שֵׁם

Read aloud two times and translate these Hebrew words:

1. שָׁלוֹם בָּרוּךְ שְׁמַע הַלְלוּיָהּ מֶלֶךְ תּוֹרָה שַׁבָּת הַשֵּׁם

Write in Hebrew the words below (include the vowels):

Hebrew	English	Hebrew	English
הַשֵּׁם	5. the Name	שָׁלוֹם	2. peace
שְׁמַע	6. hear	שַׁבָּת	3. Sabbath
מֶלֶךְ	7. king	תּוֹרָה	4. instruction

8. Write the Hebrew word for "blessed" three times:

9. Practice writing each combination six times in block or script:

כְּ

דִּ

חוּ

10. Write the English meaning:

בָּרוּךְ אַתָּה יְהוָה — Blessed (are) You Adonai

11. What are the two meanings of the Hebrew root ב.ר.ך ?
bless/kneel

12. This prayer is always chanted after the Sh'ma (Deuteronomy 6:4). Circle the word for "blessed":

(בָּרוּךְ) שֵׁם כְּבוֹד מַלְכוּתוֹ לְעוֹלָם וָעֶד:

ba-ROOKH shem k-VOD mal-**KHOO**-to l-o-LAM va-ED

Blessed is the name of His glorious kingdom for ever and ever.

13. Take the self-quiz on the next page (without looking up the answers.) Then complete your set of flashcards for lessons 1-5 and *practice, practice, practice!*

You may want to print the next page to give to students so they can check their work. Answers are also on the Lesson Fill-In page.

Lesson 5 כ ך ח   *HWJ Teacher's Guide*

Self-quiz – Lesson 5
_____שֵׁם

We are halfway through the course. *Complete this page **without** looking up the answers.*
Use your flashcards to practice those you answered incorrectly.

A. Match the letters to their sounds:

- _10_ א
- _13_ מ
- _11_ ת
- _9_ ר
- _14_ שׁ
- _8_ ך
- _12_ ן
- _15_ י

8. kh
9. r
10. silent
11. t
12. n
13. m
14. sh
15. y

B. Match the letters to their sounds:

- _5_ ה
- _7_ ם
- _3_ נ
- _1_ ח
- _2_ ע
- _6_ ל
- _4_ ב

1. kh
2. silent
3. n
4. b
5. h
6. l
7. m

C. Match the words:

- _2_ Hear
- _3_ Blessed
- _5_ Peace
- _4_ Sabbath
- _1_ The Name
- _6_ Instruction

1. הַשֵׁם
2. שְׁמַע
3. בָּרוּךְ
4. שַׁבָּת
5. שָׁלוֹם
6. תּוֹרָה

D. Match the sounds (numbers can be repeated):

- _2_ תַ
- _3_ תוֹ
- _2_ תָ
- _1_ תוּ
- _5_ תֵ
- _4_ תִי
- _5_ תֶ
- _1_ תֻ
- _6_ תְ
- _4_ תִ

1. too
2. tah
3. toe
4. tee
5. teh
6. tuh

*Answers on Lesson Fill-In page

HWJ Teacher's Guide   Lesson 5 ח ו כ

‏שֵׁם_____ Extra Challenge - Lesson 5

14. On the Shabbat Guide in this lesson, practice reading all of the prayers in Hebrew. Use the transliterations to help you with letters you don't know!

15. Before a Sabbath meal, use the Shabbat Guide to "remember the Sabbath and keep it holy." Let everyone have a part in reading the Scriptures and prayers.
This handout is just a guide – feel free to add or change any part.
Also, feel free to make copies of the Shabbat Guide to use in the future.

16. After Shabbat, write down your impressions of the experience below:

After students complete this assignment, ask 1 or 2 students to share their experience with the class.

Lesson 6 ד ב ו

> **Israeli Phrases**
> Hello/goodbye friends!   kha-ve-REEM!   שָׁלוֹם

A - Letters

Sound	Name	Letter	
"d" as in <u>d</u>oor	DA-let	ד	A1
"v" as in <u>v</u>ictory	Bet (without a dot) (BKPK letter)	ב	A2
"v" as in <u>v</u>ictory or silent as a vowel	Vav	ו	A3

Vav ו has a "v" sound if there is a vowel under it or no vowel: ו וְ וָ וּ   A4

Vav ו is silent as part of a vowel if there is a dot inside or over it: וֹ וּ   A5

Read the following line two times:

ו וַ וְ וָא בֶ בִּי דָ וּ דִי וַד   A6

Read the following line and translate:

יְיָ/יְהוָה   לֵב   תּוֹדָה   דָּוִד   אָב   A7
LORD   heart   thanks   David   father   A8
see below

יְהוָה (or the abbreviation יְיָ) is called the "unpronounceable Name of God" and is found more than six thousand times in the Scriptures! The original Hebrew did not contain vowels; therefore, there is no way to know how the Name of God should be pronounced. Hence, religiously observant Jews say the name "a-do-NAI" (my LORD) when they are in synagogue or reading their prayer books and they say the name "ha-SHEM" (the Name) at all other times. Some of the other names said in English: The LORD, Jehovah, Yehovah, Yah, Yahweh

The Hebrew name can also take many forms: יְהוָה   יְיָ   יהוה

A9

Lesson 6 ב ד

Read the following line and translate:

שׁוּב	שָׁבוּעוֹת	עִבְרִית	חֲבֵרִים	A10
turn/return	weeks	Hebrew	friends	A11

B - Prefix וּ

B1 The prefix וּ or וְ is used to add "and" before a Hebrew word: "and peace" = וְשָׁלוֹם

Read each word then write the English translation of the following:

B2 וְשָׁמַע ___and hear___   וּמֹשֶׁה ___and Moshe___

B3 In ancient Hebrew (Paleo-Hebrew), the Vav was the shape of a hook (which has the ability to "hook" things together – just like the word "and.") In fact, Torah scribes start each column with a Vav, thus "hooking" the columns together.

C - Look-Alike Letters

אוֹ אָן		בָ כָ		דָ רָ	
Vav is shorter	C3	Bet has a bottom bar	C2	Dalet has a top bar	C1

Read the following line two times:

C4 כוּ בוּ עוּ עֶן רַן רַו דִי רִי דֹח רֹה

D - Writing

	Letter	Block	Practice, then make flashcards	Script
D1	ד	ד		ד
D2	ב	ב		ב
D3	ו	ו		ו

E - Vowels

Sound	Vowel	
"a" as in <u>a</u>ll	ָ	E1
At the **beginning or middle of a word** - "kha" as in חַלָּה At the **end of a word** - "akh" as in רוּחַ (say the vowel first, then the letter)	חַ	E2

Make flashcards for the vowels above: E3

Read the following lines and translate:

עֲבוֹדָה	אַהֲבָה	רוּחַ	נֹחַ	חַלָּה	E4
work/serve/worship	love	Spirit/wind/breath	Noah	braided bread	E5

עֲלִיָּה	רַחֲמִים	מוֹעֲדִים	מָשִׁיחַ	E6
going up/immigrate to Israel	mercy/mercies	appointed times	anointed one	E7

see below

עֲלִיָּה

*Jeremiah 23:3 says "I will gather the remnant of My flock out of all the countries where I have driven them, and will bring them back to their folds, and they will be fruitful and multiply." Since the late 1800s, Jews around the world have felt drawn to "Make Al'iyah," to immigrate to Israel, the promised Jewish homeland. The word "**Aliyah**," meaning "**going up**," is a picture of going up to Jerusalem! "Aliyah" is also the word used in Jewish synagogue services for the privilege of being asked to "go up" to the "Beema" (raised platform) to recite the Hebrew prayers before and after the Torah reading.*   E8

Lesson 6 דבו   *HWJ Teacher's Guide*

F - Root

Word Meaning	Key Word	Root Meaning	Root
love (noun)	אַהֲבָה	love	א.ה.ב

F1

Write the Hebrew word for "love" then make a flashcard for the key word *and* the root: F2

Circle the root for "love":   F3

וְאָהַבְתָּ אֵת יְיָ אֱלֹהֶיךָ

v-a-**HAV**-ta et a-do-**NAI** e-lo-**HE**-kha

And you shall love the LORD your God…   Deuteronomy 6:5

G – Sing!

Write the Hebrew or English translation for the following three words:

שָׁלוֹם Good bye   חֲבֵרִים *friends*   לְהִתְרָאוֹת *see you later*   G1

Make sure that students review these 3 words many times before teaching the song.

On the internet, look up "Shalom Chaverim" on YouTube, then read and sing the Hebrew as you listen to this famous Israeli good-bye song!   G2

Before teaching the song, print many copies of the 3 Hebrew words from Shalom Chaverim (in the Teacher Resource section at the end of the book.). After teaching this song to the students, mix up the handouts and give each student one of the pages. Ask students to quickly lift up their page above their head as that word is sung.

שָׁלוֹם חֲבֵרִים!
שָׁלוֹם חֲבֵרִים!
שָׁלוֹם. שָׁלוֹם.
לְהִתְרָאוֹת! לְהִתְרָאוֹת!
שָׁלוֹם. שָׁלוֹם.

Exercises Lesson 6

שֵׁם _____

1. Read and translate these words:

שְׁמַע תּוֹרָה אַהֲבָה שַׁבָּת יהוה בָּרוּךְ שָׁלוֹם

Write the matching number under the picture:

2. עֶרֶב tov
3. שָׁלוֹם kha-ve-REEM
4. **BO**-ker tov
5. שְׁמִי ____ na-EEM m-OD.
6. **LAI**-la tov
7. שָׁבוּעַ Tov

 3  6  2

 7  4 5

8. Practice writing and saying each combination six times in block or script:

דִּ

בְּל

רָךְ

9. Write the Hebrew word for "love" three times:

_____

10. Write the Hebrew (include vowels) for the following English words (all words are in the lesson):

רוּחַ Spirit   אָב father   לֵב heart   תּוֹדָה thanks

11. What is the meaning of the Hebrew root א.ה.ב?

love

Exercises Lesson 6

12. Write 2 different Hebrew forms of the "unpronounceable" Name of God:

    יְהֹוָה   יְיָ

13. Write the English meaning below (in the lesson!): וְאָהַבְתָּ אֵת יְיָ אֱלֹהֶיךָ

    And you shall love the LORD your God

14. What does וּ or וְ mean at the beginning of a word? ____and____

15. Circle the letter ו found at the beginning of 4 words in Deuteronomy 6:5-6:

    וְאָהַבְתָּ אֵת יְהוָה אֱלֹהֶיךָ בְּכָל־לְבָבְךָ וּבְכָל־נַפְשְׁךָ
    וּבְכָל־מְאֹדֶךָ: וְהָיוּ הַדְּבָרִים הָאֵלֶּה אֲשֶׁר אָנֹכִי מְצַוְּךָ
    הַיּוֹם עַל־לְבָבֶךָ:

    And you shall love Adonai your God with all your heart and with all your soul and with all your strength. And these words which I am commanding you today (shall be) on your heart.

16. Underline the ROOT letters for "love" in the above scripture.

17. Circle the 7 key Hebrew words below: Sabbath, peace, love, instruction, hear, LORD, blessed. The words can be vertical, horizontal or diagonal.

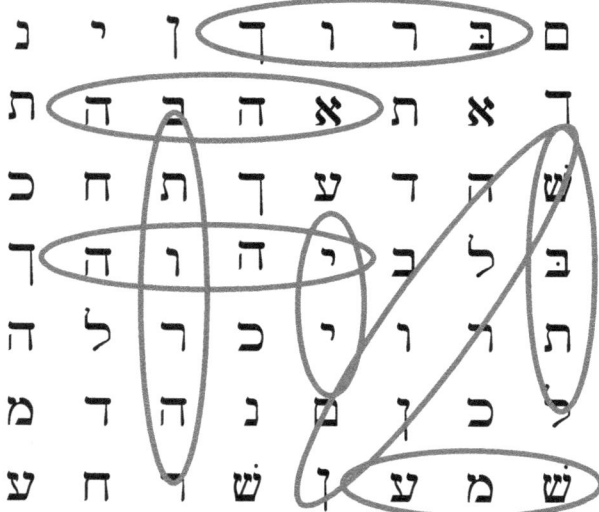

Note: 2 forms of Adonai!

Lesson 7 פ ז צ ץ

Israeli Phrases	
Thanks very much	תּוֹדָה רַבָּה
You're welcome	b-va-ka-SHA

You may want to supply a candy bar (or another gift) that can be passed in the chain drill as students practice these phrases.

A - Letters

Sound	Name	Letter	
"p" as in **p**ray	Pay (with a dot) (BKPK letter)	פּ	A1
"z" as in **z**eal	**ZA**-yin	ז	A2
"ts" as in roo**ts**	**TSA**-dee (looks like praying hands)	צ	A3
"ts" as in roo**ts**	**TSA**-dee so-**FEET** (looks like reaching to God!)	ץ	A4

Read the following line two times:

A5   צַ   צְ   וִץ   פֻּ   זִי   פֶּה   יָז   זֶה   *this/that*   עֵץ   *tree*

Look-Alike Letters

A6   עַ   צַ

Read the following line two times:

A7   עִיף   צִיף   עָן   צָן   צַם   עַם

Read the following line and translate:

A8   מְזוּזָה   מִשְׁפָּחָה   פּוּרִים   צִיצִית
A9   *doorpost/ prayer box*   *family*   *Feast of Lots*   *fringes*

A10   When an Orthodox boy turns three years old, his hair is cut for the first time and he also receives his first צִיצִית. "Speak to Bnei-Yisrael. Say to them that they are to make for themselves tzitzit on the corners of their garments throughout their generations, and they are to put a blue cord on each tzitzit. It will be your tzitzit—so whenever you look at them, you will remember all the mitzvot [commandments] of Adonai (Numbers 15:38-39)

Lesson 7   פ צ ז ץ   *HWJ Teacher's Guide*

Read the following line and try to translate:

A11   צִיּוֹן _Zion_   חֻפָּה _wedding canopy_   בַּר מִצְוָה _son of (the) commandment_ (see below)

A12   The **Bar Mitzvah** (Son of the Commandment) is the traditional coming into adulthood for a Jewish boy on his thirteenth birthday. Girls celebrate their **Bat Mitzvah** (Daughter of the Commandment) on their twelfth birthday (thirteenth birthday in Reform Judaism). The ceremony includes reading a portion of the Torah that was read on the week they were born. This author had the privilege of celebrating her Bat Mitzvah at age 62 (50 years after the normal tradition!)

B - Vowels

Sound	Vowel	
"ai" as in p<u>ie</u> ("a" + "ee") (vowel is flat like a pie ◌ַ)	יִ	B1
"ay" as in l<u>ay</u> ("e" + "ee") (the eggs ◌ֵ lay side by side)	יֵ	B2

These vowel combinations are very hard for beginners. Have them SLOWLY pronounce "a" + "ee" so they hear it makes "ai" as in pie. Do the same for "e" + "ee" to make "ay."

Make flashcards for the vowels above:

Read this line 2 times:

B3   בֵּי בִּי דִי דֵי לִי לֵי חִי זִי זֵי צִי צֵי פִּי פֵּי

Read the following lines and translate:

B4   אֱלֹהֵינוּ _our God_   בְּנֵי _sons/children (of)_   שַׁדַּי _almighty_

B5   יְרוּשָׁלַיִם _Jerusalem_   לְחַיִּים _to life_   חַיִּים _life_   חַי _live_

B6

B7   For the Jewish people, life is everything! God has protected His people and allowed them to חַי today in their own land. Each Hebrew letter is assigned a number value (called **Gematria**.) Because the number value of the letters ח (8) plus י (10) = 18, Jews traditionally tithe in multiples of 18. In the synagogue, this giving is done in ts-da-KA (charity) boxes. In fact, if you want to plant a tree in Israel, each tree costs $18!

HWJ Teacher's Guide   Lesson 7   פ צ ז ץ

Many Jewish homes have a מְזוּזָה prayer box (literally - doorpost) next to their doors to honor the Holy Scriptures placed inside. (See Deuteronomy 6:9) Some have "שׁ" on the cover which stands for שַׁדַּי - meaning "Almighty" (literally - my breast) The letters שׁדי also represent three words meaning "Guardians of the Doors of Israel!" (shom-REEM d-la-TOT yees-ra-EL) שׁוֹמְרִים דְּלָתוֹת יִשְׂרָאֵל   B8

C - Root

Meaning	Key Word	Root Meaning	Root	
life	חַיִּים	live	ח.י.ה	C1

Circle the Hebrew words meaning "Tree of Life":

עֵץ־חַיִּים הִיא לַמַּחֲזִיקִים בָּהּ   C2

ets khai-YEEM hee la-ma-kha-zee-KEEM ba

She is a tree of life to those who are strong in her. Proverbs 3:18

D - Writing

Script	Practice, then write flashcards	Block	Letter	
ð	---	פ	פ	D1
ʓ	---	ז	ז	D2
3	---	צ	צ	D3
ϙ	---	ץ	ץ	D4

 In script, the end of **TSA**-dee so-FEET goes up   D5

------------------------- Write the Hebrew word for "life" and make a flashcard   D6
------------------------- for the key word *and* the root:

Vowel Slap Game: *If you are studying in a group, one person reads a vowel sound, then two other people try to be the first to SLAP (or point to) that combination. After reading all the vowels, rotate so there is a new reader. If you are studying by yourself, point to random vowels to practice.*

If you are using the Teacher PPTs, give fly swatters to two students to "slap" the right answer. Ask another student to call out a sound.

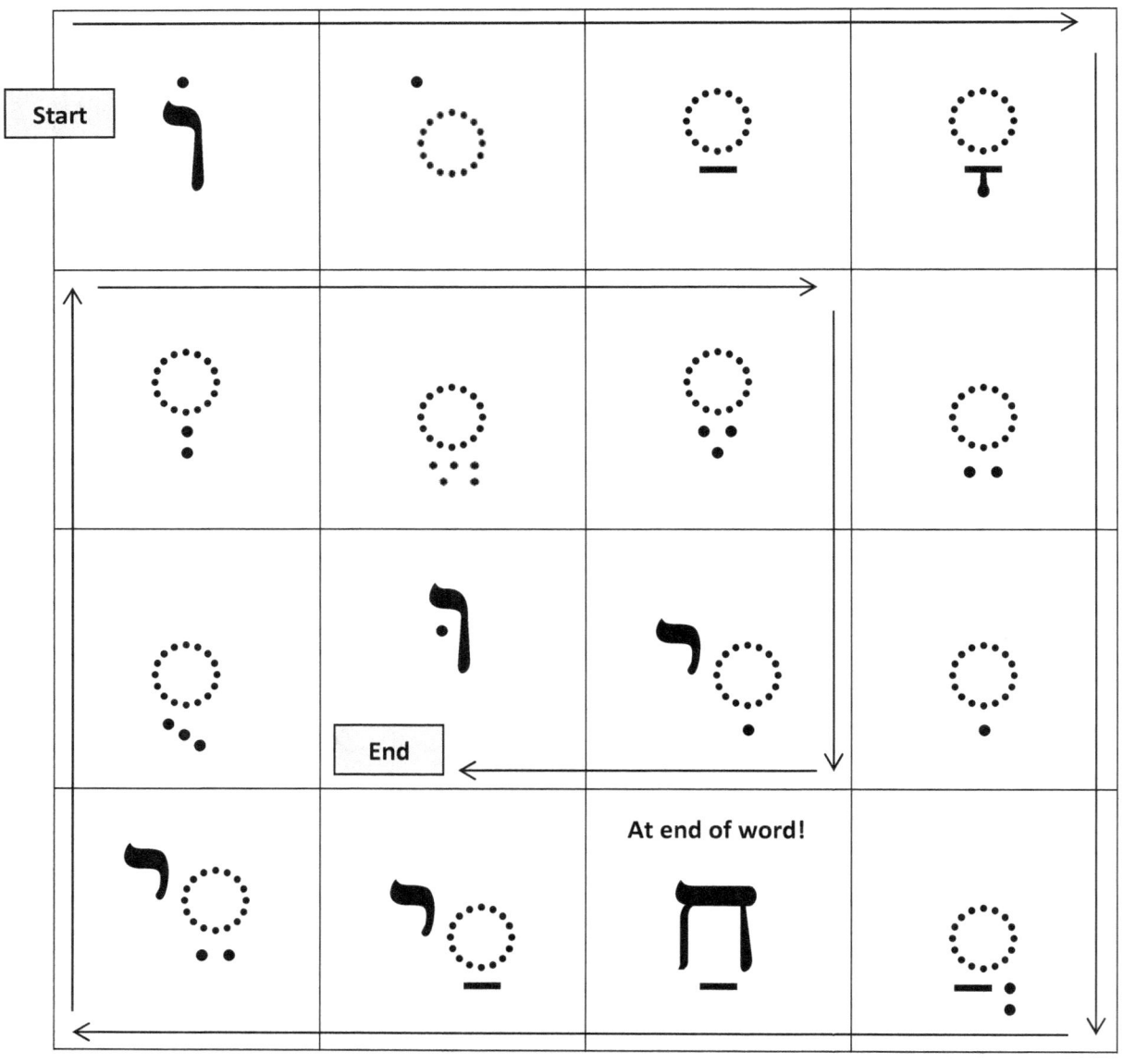

HWJ Teacher's Guide   Lesson 7   פ צ ז

Exercises Lesson 7   שֵׁם _____

1. Read and translate these words:

    יָד   בָּרוּךְ   תּוֹרָה   אַהֲבָה   שְׁמַע   חַיִּים   שָׁלוֹם

2. Complete your letter, vowel and key word flashcards through lesson 7. Memorize all letters, vowels and key words before moving to the next lesson.

3. Write the missing Hebrew or English words:

	English	Hebrew
4.	almighty	שַׁדַּי
5.	Jerusalem	יְרוּשָׁלַיִם
6.	son of (the) commandment	בַּר מִצְוָה
7.	live	חַי
8.	tree of life	עֵץ חַיִּים
9.	family	מִשְׁפָּחָה

10. Practice reading and writing each combination six times in block or script:

    צַר

    עֵץ

    זֵי

    פֵּי

11. Write the correct form of the **TSA**-dee in the following words from the lesson and write the English translation:

    צִיּוֹן ___Zion___   עֵץ ___tree___   בַּר מִצְוָה ___son of (the) commandment___

59

Exercises Lesson 7

12. What is the meaning of the Hebrew root ח.י.ה?

   _____live_____

13. Write three Hebrew words that come from the root above:

   לְחַיִּים   חַיִּים   חַי

14. This beloved Hebrew prayer based on Proverbs 3:17-18 is found In the Siddur (Jewish prayer book.) Circle the words for "tree of life" and "peace:"

עֵץ חַיִּים הִיא לַמַּחֲזִיקִים בָּה וְתֹמְכֶיהָ מְאֻשָּׁר
דְּרָכֶיהָ דַרְכֵי נֹעַם וְכָל נְתִיבוֹתֶיהָ שָׁלוֹם
הֲשִׁיבֵנוּ יהוה אֵלֶיךָ וְנָשׁוּבָה. חַדֵּשׁ יָמֵינוּ כְּקֶדֶם

"She is a tree of life to those who are strong in her and those who hold her fast will prosper [go straight]. Her ways are pleasant, and all of her paths peaceful."
(The last Hebrew line above is added in the Siddur, the Hebrew Prayer Book - "Return us to you, God, so that we shall return; renew our days as of old.")

15. In your own words, summarize Proverbs 3:13-18:

   _____
   _____
   _____
   _____
   _____

16. In the Scripture above, who is "she"? (Hint – see Proverbs 3:13):

   _____wisdom_____

Lesson 8 פ ף ק כ

Israeli Phrases
All the honor/glory! (Well done!)   kol ha-ka-VOD!

Sound	Name	Letter	
"f" as in faith	Pay (BKPK -without a dot - soft sound)	פ	A1
"f" as in faith	Pay so-FEET	ף	A2
"k" as in king	Koof	ק	A3
"k" as in king	Kaf (BKPK– with a dot - hard sound)	כ	A4

A - Letters

Read the following lines two times:

A5   כִּיף   כֵּיק   עַף   כִּיף   קוֹ   קוּ   פַּ   פְּ   פֵּ

A6   כִּי   פוּק   כִּין   עוּק   שִׁיךְ   לוּף   הַם   צֵךְ

Read the following lines and try to translate:

A7   שׁוֹפָר *ram's horn*   קְהִילָה community/congregation   צְדָקָה charity   נֶפֶשׁ soul   כָּבוֹד honor/glory
A8

A9   חֲנֻכָּה *Feast of Dedication*   תְּפִלָּה prayer   יוֹם כִּפּוּר *Day of Atonement*   הַתִּקְוָה the Hope (see below)
A10

A11   הַתִּקְוָה (The Hope) was a poem written in 1878, inspired by the Zionist movement (Jews returning to the Promised Land). It was not until 2004 that the Israeli government officially designated הַתִּקְוָה as Israel's national anthem. Today, this song is sung with tears of joy because, after centuries, יְהוָה has brought His chosen people home to freedom! Psalm 37:9 promises that "those who **hope** in the LORD will inherit the land."

Lesson 8 כ ק ף פ　　　　　　　　　　　　　　　　　　　　　HWJ Teacher's Guide

Play HaTikva from a CD or from the Internet on YouTube. The tradition is to stand to honor Israel's national anthem.

HaTikva

A12

כֹּל עוֹד בַּלֵּבָב פְּנִימָה נֶפֶשׁ יְהוּדִי הוֹמִיָּה
וּלְפַאֲתֵי מִזְרָח, קָדִימָה עַיִן לְצִיּוֹן צוֹפִיָּה
עוֹד לֹא אָבְדָה תִּקְוָתֵנוּ, הַתִּקְוָה בַּת שְׁנוֹת אַלְפַּיִם
לִהְיוֹת עַם חָפְשִׁי בְּאַרְצֵנוּ אֶרֶץ צִיּוֹן וִירוּשָׁלַיִם.

kol od ba-le-VAV p-nee-MA, **NE**-fesh y-**HOO**-dee ho-mee-YA
ool-fa-a-TAY meez-RAKH ka-dee-MA, a-YEEN l-tsee-YON tso-fee-YA
od lo av-DA teek-va-**TAY**-noo, ha-teek-VA bat sh-not al-**PAI**-yeem
lee-YOT am khof-SHEE b-ar-**TSAY**-noo, **E**-rets tsee-YON vee-roo-sha-**LAI**-yeem

As long as in the heart, within, a Jewish soul still yearns,
And onward, toward the ends of the east, an eye still gazes toward Zion;
Our hope is not yet lost, the hope of two thousand years,
To be a free people in our land, the land of Zion and Jerusalem.

B - Writing

Script	Practice then make flashcards	Block	Letter	
᎒		פּ	פ	B1
ᶠ		ף	ף	B2
ק		ק	ק	B3
ᴐ		כּ	כ	B4

*In script, the end of **TSA**-dee so**FEET** goes up and the Pay so-**FEET** goes down.* B5

62

C - Root

Word Meaning	Key Word	Root Meaning	Root	
holy	קָדוֹשׁ	holy, set apart	ק.ד.שׁ	C1

C2   קִדּוּשׁ   Sanctification - Shabbat Blessing over the Wine (in Lesson 5)

Read and translate:

C3   רוּחַ הַקוֹדֶשׁ   __Spirit__   __Holy__

C4   Write the Hebrew word for "holy" then make a flashcard for the key word *and* the root:

*Be sure to pronounce "Holy Spirit" correctly: **ROO**-akh ha-**KO**-desh. Notice the accents on both words.*

D - Exception Vowel

Example	Sound	Vowel	
כָּל = kol	"**o**" as in fl**ow**	ָ	D1

D2   Make a flashcard noting that it is an "exception" vowel:

D3   כָּל   all/everything   (כָּל sounds like "kol")

D4   כָּל הַכָּבוֹד   All the honor/glory! (Well done!)

D5   הַכָּל b-**SE**-der   "the all" is in order (everything's OK)

D6   כָּל־הָאָרֶץ   All (of) the earth   (כָּל sounds like "khol")

D7   Read and translate the words you know:

קָדוֹשׁ קָדוֹשׁ קָדוֹשׁ יְהוָה צְבָאוֹת
מְלֹא כָל־הָאָרֶץ כְּבוֹדוֹ:

*"Holy, holy, holy, is Adonai - The LORD of hosts!
The whole earth is full of His glory." Isaiah 6:3*

HWJ Teacher's Guide   Lesson 8   כ ק ף פ

Group Memory Game – *Cut or photocopy this page, then cut out the pieces. Place the pieces on a table with the words facing down and mix well. Player 1 turns over two cards to see if they match (Hebrew with English meaning.) If they do, player 1 keeps the pair and turns over two more. If they don't match, player 2 takes a turn. Play continues until all pairs are matched. Player with the most pairs wins.*

שְׁמַע	life	תּוֹרָה
blessed	קָדוֹשׁ	love
יְהוָה	instruction	holy
hear	שַׁבָּת	LORD
אַהֲבָה	Sabbath	שָׁלוֹם
חַיִּים	בָּרוּךְ	peace

HWJ Teacher's Guide Lesson 8 כ ק פ

_____ שֵׁם # Exercises Lesson 8

Rearrange the letters and vowels in the following **key** words.
In the chart, write the correct Hebrew words and their English translations:

English translation	Key Hebrew Word		
love	אַהֲבָה	בְּאַהֲ	1.
life	חַיִּים	יִּחַם	2.
instruction	תּוֹרָה	רָתוֹ	3.
Sabbath	שַׁבָּת	תבַּשׁ	4.
blessed	בָּרוּךְ	וּרךְבָּ	5.
holy	קָדוֹשׁ	דקָשׁוֹ	6.
peace	שָׁלוֹם	וֹמשָׁל	7.
hear	שְׁמַע	משְׁע	8.

9. Practice reading and writing each combination five times in block or script:

כָּל
כִּי
פִּי
עָף

Write the correct form of Pay in the following words then translate to English:

10. נֶפֶשׁ soul   שׁוֹפָר ram's horn   אָלֶף Alef

11. What is the English meaning of כָּל? _all/everything_

12. Write in *Hebrew* the name for the Israeli National Anthem: הַתִּקְוָה

13. Write in *English* the name for the Israeli National Anthem: The Hope

67

Exercises Lesson 8

Kadosh

by Elisheva Shomrom (from Isaiah 6:3)
English words by Paul Wilbur

Listen to a version of "Kadosh" (on YouTube) then fill in the missing Hebrew and English words below: (Notice that each line is repeated twice!)

14.

עִבְרִית

	קָדוֹשׁ	קָדוֹשׁ	קָדוֹשׁ
	קָדוֹשׁ	קָדוֹשׁ	קָדוֹשׁ
	צְבָאוֹת	אֱלֹהִים	יְהוָה
	צְבָאוֹת	אֱלֹהִים	יְהוָה
וְיָבוֹא	וְהֹוֶה	הָיָה	אֲשֶׁר
וְיָבוֹא	וְהֹוֶה	הָיָה	אֲשֶׁר

English

Holy	holy	holy	
holy	holy	holy	
(O) LORD	(our) God	(LORD of) Hosts	
(O) LORD	(our) God	(LORD of) Hosts	
Who	was	and (who) is	and (who) is to come
Who	was	and (who) is	and (who) is to come

Lesson 9 שׁ ס ט ג

> **Israeli Phrase**
> Happy Holiday!   khag sa-**ME**-akh!

A - Letters

Sound	Name	Letter	
"s" as in **s**on	Shin (dot on the left)	שׁ	A1
"s" as in **s**on	**SA**-mekh	ס	A2
"t" as in **t**op (has a *top* hole)	Tet	ט	A3
"g" as in **g**ap (has a *gap*)	**GI**-mel	ג	A4

Notice the high-heeled gap!

Read the following lines two times:

A5   שֶׁ שָׁ סִי סוּ טוּ טִי עָג אִיט

A6   שִׁים סוֹט טַי גִין סִי גִץ סַג גוּת טָךְ

Read and translate the following two lines:

A7   סֻכּוֹת   פֶּסַח   סֵדֶר   טוֹב   חֶסֶד

A8   Feast of Tabernacles | Passover | order | good | kindness

A9   טַלִּית   טָהוֹר   עֹנֶג שַׁבָּת   יִשְׂרָאֵל

A10   prayer shawl | clean/pure | Sabbath delight | Israel

A11   The original meaning of יִשְׂרָאֵל "Israel" comes from two roots: שׂ.ר.ה "to persevere, have power, strive or contend" and א.ל "God." Only through the power of our Mighty God has Israel persevered for more than two thousand years!

Lesson 9   ג ט ס ש   HWJ Teacher's Guide

Read the following Scripture:

לֵב טָהוֹר בְּרָא־לִי אֱלֹהִים   A12

Create in me a clean heart, O God   Psalm 51:12

מוֹעֲדִים

Leviticus 23:2 "Speak to the sons of Israel and tell them, '"These are my appointed times, the festivals of Adonai, which you are to proclaim to be sacred assemblies."' Scripture is clear about these מוֹעֲדִים "God Appointments" on His holy calendar. They are to be eternal reminders of His faithfulness to us. Translate these and share what they represent: A13

שָׁבוּעוֹת   שַׁבָּת   סֻכּוֹת   פֶּסַח

B - Vowels

Sound: "ooey" as in g**ooey**	וּי	B1
Sound: "oy" as in t**oy** or "**oy** vay!" (Yiddish for "Oh my goodness!")	וֹי	B2

Make flashcards for the above vowel combinations: B3

Read and translate:

gentiles/nations   גּוֹיִים   gentile/nation   גּוֹי   worthy   רָאוּי   B4

You are worthy   אַתָּה רָאוּי   B5

C - Root

Word Meaning	Key Word	Root Meaning	Root	
joy	שִׂמְחָה	joyful	שׂ.מ.ח	C1

Read and translate:

joy (of) Torah   שִׂמְחַת תּוֹרָה   C2

שִׂמְחַת תּוֹרָה

is celebrated on the eighth day of סֻכּוֹת (Feast of Tabernacles). During this joyous holiday, the Torah scroll readings are finished for the year and the Torah is rolled back to the beginning (Gen. 1:1) to start a new yearly cycle. The men dance around the Torah and carry it through the neighborhood. It is indeed a joyous celebration of God's Holy Word!   C3

Review these 2 words that were already taught at the beginning of this lesson.

(happy) שָׂמֵחַ _____ חַג (holiday)

When greeting someone during a holiday in Israel, it is customary to add the name of the holiday between "khag" and "sa-**ME**-akh"
Read and translate the following greetings:

חַג סֻכּוֹת שָׂמֵחַ!

חַג פֶּסַח שָׂמֵחַ!

חַג חֲנֻכָּה שָׂמֵחַ!

C4

D - Writing

Script	Practice then make flashcards	Block	Letter	
ש (script)		שׁ	שׁ	D1
ס (script)		ס	ס	D2
ט (script)		ט	ט	D3
ג (script)		ג	ג	D4

Write the Hebrew word for "joy" then make a flashcard for the key word *and* the root.   D5

Match the Roots and Key Words! *Make two copies of Game Page 1 and Page 2. Cut out the pieces and give each team a complete set. The teams turn the pieces face down on a table. On a signal from the leader, teams turn over all of the pieces and try to match the root, meaning of the root, key Hebrew word from the root & English meaning of the word. First team to match all 9 sets wins the game.*

Game Page 1

joyful	שַׁבָּת	hit the mark
ש.ל.ם	ב.ר.ך	completion, wholeness
life	תּוֹרָה	blessed
ש.מ.ע	שְׁמַע	hear & obey
חַיִּים	בָּרוּךְ	rest, stop
א.ה.ב	peace	שִׂמְחָה

Game Page 2

ח.י.ה	love	live
instruction	אַהֲבָה	holy
שׂ.מ.ח	bless, kneel	י.ר.ה
ק.ד.שׁ	holy	Joy
Sabbath	שׁ.ב.ת	קָדוֹשׁ
hear	שָׁלוֹם	love

Lesson 9 שׁ ס ט ג

Exercises Lesson 9 שֵׁם ‎_____

1. Read and translate these Hebrew words:

בָּרוּךְ תּוֹרָה אַהֲבָה שַׁבָּת יְהוָה שָׁלוֹם רוּחַ
חַיִּים קָדוֹשׁ שְׁמַע שִׂמְחָה יִשְׂרָאֵל

2. Write the English letter that matches the עִבְרִית:

A. Happy holiday	
B. Good morning	
C. Sabbath peace	
D. Thanks a lot. You're welcome.	
E. My name is Dan. Nice to meet you.	
F. Holy Spirit	
G. All the honor/glory	
H. Blessed are you, LORD.	
I. Hear, Israel	
J. Hello/Goodbye friends	

G	כָּל הַכָּבוֹד
C	שַׁבָּת שָׁלוֹם
I	שְׁמַע יִשְׂרָאֵל
E	שְׁמִי דָן. נָעִים מְאֹד.
B	בּוֹקֶר טוֹב
A	חַג שָׂמֵחַ
D	תּוֹדָה רַבָּה. בְּבַקָּשָׁה
J	שָׁלוֹם חֲבֵרִים
H	בָּרוּךְ אַתָּה יְהוָה
F	רוּחַ הַקוֹדֶשׁ

3. Write the key words in Hebrew:

תּוֹרָה	instruction	חַיִּים	life
אַהֲבָה	love	יְיָ, יְהוָה, יהוה	LORD
שַׁבָּת	Sabbath	בָּרוּךְ	blessed
שְׁמַע	hear	שָׁלוֹם	peace
שִׂמְחָה	joy	קָדוֹשׁ	holy

4. Write the *root* letters meaning "joy"   ‎שׂ.מ.ח

5. Write the Hebrew for "Happy holiday!"   חַג שָׂמֵחַ

6. Complete your flashcard set for all the letters, vowels and key words Practice them every day until you know them by heart!

Exercises Lesson 9

Fill in the missing English translations:

אוֹתְךָ!	אוֹהֵב	אֲנִי	אַבָּא	שָׁלוֹם	Man writing to his Father	7.
you (m)	love (m)	I	Daddy	Hello		
אוֹתְךָ	אוֹהֶבֶת	אֲנִי	אַבָּא	שָׁלוֹם	Woman writing to her Father	8.
you (m)	love (f)	I	Daddy	hello		

Practice your עִבְרִית by writing the prayer above in Hebrew:
(If you are a man, write line 7 from above, if you are a woman, write line 8)

9. עִבְרִית _____

Extra Challenge

10. Write your own new Hebrew prayer to Adonai! Try to use as many Hebrew words as you can! Refer to the Dictionary in the Appendix to help you:

_____
_____
_____

After doing the homework, ask 1 or 2 students to share their prayers with the class.

11. Translate your prayer into English:

_____
_____
_____

HWJ Teacher's Guide
Reading Scriptures

Lesson 10
Reading Scriptures

Syllable lines are especially helpful with big words!

A – Syllable Breaks

To help read Hebrew words, add syllable lines to the Scripture – one sounded vowel per syllable	A1
בָּ\רוּךְ הַ\בָּא בְּ\שֵׁם יְיָ*	A2
*Syllable marks are not used in the unpronounceable name of God	A3

Assign each of these scriptures to 2 students to work on together before they present it to the class.

Add syllable lines then read the Scriptures:

זָכוֹר אֶת־יוֹם הַשַּׁבָּת לְקַדְּשׁוֹ   A4

Remember the Sabbath day to keep it holy. (Exodus 20:8)

יֵצֶר סָמוּךְ תִּצֹּר שָׁלוֹם שָׁלוֹם   A5

You keep in perfect peace one whose mind is stayed on You. (Isaiah 26:3)

עֵץ־חַיִּים הִיא לַמַּחֲזִיקִים בָּהּ   A6

She is a tree of life to those who embrace her. (Proverbs 3:18)

לֵב טָהוֹר בְּרָא־לִי אֱלֹהִים   A7

Create in me a clean heart, O God. (Psalm 51:12(10))

גַּל־עֵינַי וְאַבִּיטָה נִפְלָאוֹת מִתּוֹרָתֶךָ:   A8

Open my eyes, so I may behold wonders from Your Torah. (Psalm 119:18)

Lesson 10
Reading Scriptures

HWJ Teacher's Guide

B – Cantillation Accent Marks

*The special markings in Biblical Hebrew are called "**Cantillation Marks**." They have three purposes: First, they show the accented syllable of each word. Second, they divide verses into smaller units of meaning and put phrases together. Last, the marks have a musical value allowing the "Cantors" (song leaders) to chant the verses.*	B1

When you are pronouncing a Hebrew word from the Scriptures, there could be many cantillation marks. One of them shows the accented syllable.	B2
גַּל־עֵינַי וְאַבִּיטָה נִפְלָאוֹת מִתּוֹרָתֶךָ׃	B3

Read out loud the Scripture below. Use syllable lines and the accent marks to help you pronounce the Hebrew correctly.

B4

עִבְדוּ אֶת־יְהוָה בְּשִׂמְחָה

Serve/work for/worship ADONAI *with joy!* (Psalm 100:2)

*The root for "serve," ע.ב.ד also means "work" and "worship". Everything we do in life, as we work, serve or worship, should always be our very best effort for our wonderful LORD...<u>and</u> it should be done with JOY!	B5

HWJ Teacher's Guide
Reading Scriptures

Lesson 10

C – Continuing Your Hebrew!

Using your flashcards, continue to practice the letters, vowels, key words and roots you have learned.   C1

As you study the Scriptures, when you come to a verse that stands out, read it out loud in Hebrew.   C2

To welcome in the Shabbat on Friday evening (Erev Shabbat), read the Hebrew prayers on the Shabbat Handout in Chapter 5.   C3

During your quiet times, write a Hebrew prayer to Adonai in your journal. Use the dictionary in this book to help you.   C4

Use a Hebrew Bible or online Hebrew Bible program to find your favorite Scripture. Then read and write it in Hebrew as a blessing to Adonai.   C5

Use the Hebrew with Joy! Video Lessons to reinforce what you have learned. The videos can be purchased at: https://hebrewwithjoy.com/hebrew-with-joy-video-lessons/   C6

Review the Hebrew Resources page and add a new Hebrew or Bible app or program to your phone or computer.   C7

Teach others how to learn Hebrew! This is the best way to reinforce what you have learned. Please share your new knowledge by teaching others who heave a heart for God, His Land and His People! The Video lessons (link above) can be helpful for teaching individuals, families, home school, bible study or other groups.   C8

Teaching others is the best way to go deeper in your Hebrew. Remind students that there are videos and Teacher PowerPoint presentations to help in the process. Refer them to HebrewWithJoy.com to order these resources.

Lesson 10
Reading Scriptures

HWJ Teacher's Guide

Make 1 copy on colored cardstock, then cut all the lines. Pass out one line to each student or pair of students to work on. Then ask the students to read the answers.

Praise Puzzle: *Each Hebrew combination below sounds like an English word. As you sound each one out, write the English words in the left column, then read the sentences in English.*

My...best friend	מַי בֶּסְט פְּרֶנְד	1
Who is my best friend?	הוּא אִז מַי בֶּסְט פְּרֶנְד?	2
He helps me to grow.	הִע הֶלְפְּס מִיא תֶע גְרוֹה.	3
He hears my voice.	הִע הִירְז מַי בוֹיש.	4
He likes me a lot.	הִע לַיקְס מִיא אֵי לָט.	5
He holds my head up.	הִע הוֹלְדְז מַי הֶד אַפּ.	6
He never leaves me.	הִע נֶוֶר לִיבְז מִיא.	7
He guides my steps.	הִע גַיְדְז מַי שְׁטֶפְּס.	8
Do you know who my best friend is?	דֶע יוּא נוֹה הוּא מַי בֶּסְט פְּרֶנְד אִז?	9
He is my LORD, God of my heart!	הִע אִז מַי לוֹרְד, גַד אָב מַי הָרְת!	10

82

HWJ Teacher's Guide
Reading Scriptures

Lesson 10

כָּל הַכָּבוֹד!

Well done! You have now learned to read and write עִבְרִית. May Hebrew truly be a JOY as you go deeper in your study of the Hebrew Scriptures with God's Holy Language!

Graduation Suggestions:

1. Print a graduation certificate for every student with their name, teacher name and date of graduation. Refer to the HWJ Graduation certificate in the Teacher Resource section of the book. You can also go to the www.HebrewWithJoy.com website under Teachers to find a link to a Graduation certificate.

2. If possible, ask students to bring food and have a graduation party on the last class.

3. After teaching the last lesson, refer students once again to the Appendix section. Highlight the Phrase list and the Dictionary.

4. Play the graduation song while you hand out certificates (you can find Pomp & Circumstance on the Internet.)

5. Be sure to have students complete the Post-Quiz to see how much they have learned! (You may want to hand out their Pre-Quiz so they can really see their improvement!)

6. Ask students to complete the Evaluation so that you know what worked and what still needs work!

7. Ask students to review the Hebrew with Joy! book on Amazon.

8. Take a class picture and email a copy to all students. Send a copy to Hebrewwithjoy33@gmail.com to include in our class pictures.

You may want to make copies of the Post Quiz answers on the next page, then ask students to check their work. Also, refer them to the Pre-Quiz so they can see how much they have learned.

Lesson 10
Reading Scriptures

HWJ Teacher's Guide

**Please complete this page without looking up any answers.
After checking your answers, compare this quiz to the Pre-Quiz.

Name: _____

Date: _____

Post-Quiz

A. Was this your first Hebrew class? _____

B. Match the letters to their sounds:

ע _3_   1. d

צ _6_   2. r

פּ _7_   3. silent

ר _2_   4. s

ק _5_   5. k

ד _1_   6. ts

ס _4_   7. p

C. Match the sounds:

תַ _4_   1. too

תוֹ _5_   2. tee

תָ _2_   3. tie

תוּ _1_   4. tah

תַי _3_   5. toe

תִי _7_   6. teh

תֵ _6_   7. tay

D. Match the words:

שְׁמַע _4_   1. life

קָדוֹשׁ _3_   2. blessed

חַיִּים _1_   3. holy

בָּרוּךְ _2_   4. hear

E. Match the roots:

שׂ.מ.ח _3_   1. hit the mark

י.ר.ה _1_   2. love

שׁ.ב.ת _4_   3. joy

א.ה.ב _2_   4. rest/stop

E. Write in Hebrew: Sabbath Peace   שַׁבָּת שָׁלוֹם!

HWJ Teacher's Guide
Reading Scriptures

Hebrew With Joy!
Class Evaluation

> This feedback will help you in future classes.

If you are a part of a class, give or email a copy of this evaluation to your instructor and send a copy to hebrewwithjoy33@gmail.com. Todah rabah! Also, if you are studying on your own, would you be willing to write a book review that would encourage others to buy the book? Please post it through Amazon.com. Todah!

> Please ask students to post a review on Amazon.com. This will help others find the HWJ book more easily.

1. How would you rate this class on a scale of 1 to 5 (5 being the highest) _____

2. What did you like most about the class?

3. What suggestion/s do you have that would make the class better?

4. Would you be willing to write a book review that would encourage others to buy the book? Please post it through Amazon.com (search for: Hebrew with Joy!: Learn Simple Hebrew with the Scriptures)

Appendix

Lesson Fill-Ins

Fill-Ins from right to left!	Line	Lesson
daughter	B7	1
Sabbath	B11	1
peace/ hello/goodbye	B4	2
LORD, day, instruction	A7	3
name	D5	3
Moses, the name	D8	3
the peace, the Sabbath, the instruction	E2	3
God/god, son, Daddy, amen/so be it	A8	4
see you later, candlestick/lamp, Solomon	C12	4
God, hear/listen	C15	4
Rachel, king	A7	5
Ruth, hallelujah, blessed	D6	5
David, thanks	A8	6
weeks, Hebrew, friends	A11	6
and hear, and Moshe	B2	6
braided bread, spirit/wind/breath	E5	6
appointed times, going up/immigrate to Israel	E7	6
שָׁלוֹם, friends, see you later!	G1	6
tree	A5	7
doorpost/prayer box, Feast of Lots	A9	7
Zion, son of (the) commandment	A11	7
our God	B4	7
Jerusalem, to life, life	B6	7
ram's horn	A8	8
Feast of Dedication, Day of Atonement, the hope	A10	8
Holy Spirit	C3	8
Feast of Tabernacles, Passover, good	A8	9
Sabbath delight, Israel	A10	9
gentile/nation, gentiles/nations	B4	9
You are worthy	B5	9
Joy (of) Torah	C2	9
זָכוֹר אֶת־יוֹם הַשַּׁבָּת לְקַדְּשׁוֹ	A4	10
צֵר סָמוּךְ תִּצֹּר שָׁלוֹם שָׁלוֹם	A5	10
עֵץ־חַיִּים הִיא לַמַּחֲזִיקִים בָּהּ	A6	10
לֵב טָהוֹר בְּרָא־לִי אֱלֹהִים	A7	10
גַּל־עֵינַי וְאַבִּיטָה נִפְלָאוֹת מִתּוֹרָתֶךָ׃	A8	10
עִבְדוּ אֶת־יְהוָה בְּשִׂמְחָה	B4	10

Lesson 5
Answers to Self-Quiz
(from top to bottom)
A. 10,13,11,9, 14,8,12,15
B. 5,7,3,1,2,6,4
C. 2,3,5,4,1,6
D. 2,3,2,1,5,4, 5,1,6,4

Lesson 10-Praise Puzzle
1. My Best Friend
2. Who is my best friend?
3. He helps me to grow
4. He hears my voice
5. He likes me a lot
6. He holds my head up
7. He never leaves me
8. He guides my steps
9. Do you know who my best friend is?
10. He is my LORD, God of my heart

Exercise Answers:
Link:
HebrewWithJoy.com/
hwj-exercise-answers
PW: answers

Hebrew Letters

Sound	Name	Script	Block	Letter
silent	**A**-lef			א
b as in **b**ar	Bet (with a dot)			בּ
v as in **v**ictory	Bet (without a dot)			ב
g as in **g**ap	**GI**-mel			ג
d as in **d**oor	**DA**-let			ד
h as in **h**oly	Hay			ה
v as in **v**ictory	Vav			ו
z as in **z**eal	**ZA**-yin			ז
kh as in Ba**ch**	Khet			ח
t as in **t**op	Tet			ט
y as in **y**es	Yud/Yod			י
k as in **k**ing	Kaf (with a dot)			כּ
kh as in Ba**ch**	Kaf (without a dot)			כ
kh as in Ba**ch**	Kaf so-FEET			ך
l as in **l**ight	**LA**-med			ל
m as in **m**olehill	Mem			מ
m as in **m**olehill	Mem so-FEET			ם
n as in **n**ame	Nun			נ
n as in **n**ame	Nun so-FEET			ן

Hebrew Letters (cont.)

Sound	Name	Script	Block	Letter
s as in **s**on	**SA**-mekh			ס
silent	**AY**-in			ע
p as in **p**ray	Pay (with a dot)			פּ
f as in **f**aith	Pay (without a dot)			פ
f as in **f**aith	Pay so-FEET			ף
ts as in roo**ts**	**TSA**-dee			צ
ts as in roo**ts**	**TSA**-dee so-FEET			ץ
k as in **k**ing	Koof			ק
r as in **r**est	Raysh			ר
sh as in **sh**ine	Shin			שׁ
s as in **s**on	Shin			שׂ
t as in **t**oe	Tav			ת

Hebrew Vowels

"a" as in <u>a</u>ll	ָ ַ ֲ
"o" as in <u>o</u>ver (dot is **o**ver the letter)	וֹ ֹ
"e" as in <u>e</u>gg (2,3 or 5 **e**ggs in a basket)	ֱ ֵ ֶ
"ee" as in f<u>ee</u>t (the vowel is under the f<u>ee</u>t of the letter)	ִי ִ
silent or "uh" as in <u>a</u>bove (one dot **a**bove the other)	ְ
"oo" as in t<u>oo</u> ("**oo**h- it hurts)	וּ ֻ
"akh" as in B<u>ach</u> (exception – at the end of a word)	ַח
"ay" as in l<u>ay</u> ("e" + "ee")	ֵי
"ai" as in p<u>ie</u> ("a" + "ee")	ַי
"o" as in fl<u>ow</u> (exception vowel!)	ׇ
"oy" as in t<u>oy</u>	וֹי
"ooey" as in g<u>ooey</u>	וּי

Hebrew Phrases

Less #	Lesson Phrases			Classroom Phrases		
	English	Transliteration	Hebrew	English	Transliteration	Hebrew
1	hello, goodbye, peace	sha-LOM	שָׁלוֹם	class	kee-TA	כִּיתָּה
1	my name is _____	sh-mee _____.	שְׁמִי _____.	correct	na-KHON	נָכוֹן
2	nice to meet you	na-EEM m-OD	נָעִים מְאוֹד	excellent	me-tsoo-YAN	מְצוּיָן
2	see you later	l-heet-ra-OT	לְהִתְרָאוֹת	finished	ZE-o	זֶהוּ
3	good morning	BO-ker tov	בּוֹקֶר טוֹב	good	tov	טוֹב
3	good evening	E-rev tov	עֶרֶב טוֹב	great!/terrific	YO-fee	יֹפִי
3	good night	LAI-la tov	לַיְלָה טוֹב	in Hebrew	b-eev-REET	בְּעִבְרִית
3	have a good week	sha-VOO-a tov	שָׁבוּעַ טוֹב	no	lo	לֹא
4	how's it going?	ma neesh-MA?	מַה נִשְׁמַע?	quiet!	SHE-ket!	שֶׁקֶט!
4	good, thanks	tov, to-DA!	טוֹב, תּוֹדָה.	quiet, please!	SHE-ket b-va-ka-SHA!	שֶׁקֶט בְּבַקָשָׁה!
4	morning light	BO-ker or	בּוֹקֶר אוֹר	students	tal-mee-DEEM	תַלְמִידִים
5	OK, fine	b-SE-der	בְּסֵדֶר	teacher (FS)	mo-RA	מוֹרָה
6	hello, friends bye, friends	sha-LOM kha-ve-REEM	שָׁלוֹם חֲבֵרִים	teacher (MS)	mo-RE	מוֹרֶה
7	thanks very much	to-DA ra-BA	תּוֹדָה רַבָּה	very good	tov m-OD	טוֹב מְאוֹד
7	you're welcome (please)	b-va-ka-SHA	בְּבַקָשָׁה	what's this/that?	ma ze?	מַה זֶה?
8	all the honor/glory (well done)	kol ha-ka-VOD!	כָּל הַכָּבוֹד	yes	ken	כֵּן
9	happy holiday!	khag sa-ME-akh!	חַג שָׂמֵחַ!			

Hebrew Resources

1. **Blue Letter Bible -** www.blueletterbible.org Free app for phone or computer; has user friendly verse look-up with large easy-to-read Hebrew interlinear (includes vowels!)

2. **Bible Hub -** www.biblehub.com Free app for phone or computer; includes an interlinear option where you can see the Hebrew text with vowels, English word-for-word translation and Strong's concordance

3. **iTranslate -** https://www.itranslate.com Free app that translates English to Hebrew –Free App for Iphone or Ipad *includes Hebrew voice translation.*

4. **Google Translate -** https://translate.google.com Free app for phone or computer

5. **Prolog Hebrew-English Dictionary -** http://learnhebrew.prolog.co.il
   Free app for phone or computer - There is a charge for the complete dictionary
   includes vowels, accents and genders

6. **Bible Gateway -** https://www.biblegateway.com/
   Free Bible program for phone or computer; search for specific Scriptures
   Hebrew translations can be seen side-by-side next to the English!
   A Westminster Leningrad Codex (WLC) for the Tanach (Old Testament)
   B HaBrit HaKhadasha/HaDereck (HHH) for the Brit Khadashah (New Testament)

7. **Serve-A-Verse -** http://www.levsoftware.com/SAV/login.php
   Free version - Choose single verses to hear the Hebrew audio. Paid version – more options

8. **YouVersion –** https://www.youversion.com/the-bible-app/
   Free Bible app for cell phone or computer with same Hebrew translations as Bible Gateway

9. **Touch Bible -** https://www.touchbible.com/touch-bible-loaded
   Free app for cell phone –Bible with Strong's Concordance with roots, Hebrew spelling and vowels

10. **Download Hebrew Fonts –** http://www.tyndale.cam.ac.uk/unicode
    To see an on-screen computer keyboard for typing Hebrew letters and vowels

11. **Hebrew KB –** app for phone that lets you see a Hebrew keyboard and type Hebrew letters and vowels

Scriptural and Cultural Treasures Index

Scriptural and Cultural Treasures	Line	Lesson
Alef	A5	4
Aliyah	E8	6
Bar Mitzvah	A12	7
B'resheet In the Beginning	A4	1
Blessed are You Adonai	E10	5
B'reet Mila - Circumcision	C13	4
Cantillation Marks	B1	10
Chanukah Dreidel Letters	A7	2
HaTikva - National Anthem	A11	8
Hay - Holy Spirit	E3	3
Hay - Open door	A4	3
Holiday Greetings	C4	9
Israel	A11	9
Jerusalem	D3	2
Khai - live	B7	7
Khet - Life	A5	5
Mezuzah	B8	7
Midrash	B4	3
Moadeem - Appointed times	A13	9
Paleo - Hebrew	D7	2
Serve - ע.ב.ד.	B5	10
Sh'ma	D3	4
Shabbat	C7	1
Shabbat Guide		5
Shabbat Shalom Paleo Hebrew	D7	2
Shalom Chaverim song	G2	6
Simkhat Torah	C3	9
Tzitzit - Fringes	A10	7
Unpronounceable Name of God	A9	6
Vav hook	B3	6

Hebrew Dictionary

Less #	English	Transliteration	Hebrew	Less #	English	Transliteration	Hebrew
8	all/everything	kol, khol	כָּל, כֹּל	7	fringes	tsee-tseet	צִיצִית
7	almighty (my breast)	sha-DAI	שַׁדַּי	9	gentile, nation	goy	גּוֹי
4	amen - so be it	a-MEN	אָמֵן	9	gentiles, nations	go-YEEM	גּוֹיִם
6	anointed one	ma-SHEE-akh	מָשִׁיחַ	4	God, god	e-lo-HEEM, el	אֱלֹהִים אֵל
6	appointed times	mo-a-DEEM	מוֹעֲדִים	4	God/my Master	a-do-NAI	אֲדוֹנָי
5	blessed	ba-ROOKH	בָּרוּךְ	6	going up-Aliyah	a-lee-YA	עֲלִיָּה
5	blessing	bra-KHA	בְּרָכָה	9	good	tov	טוֹב
8	blessing over the wine	kee-DOOSH	קִדּוּשׁ	3	good evening	E-rev tov	עֶרֶב טוֹב
9	booths, Feast of Tabernacles	soo-KOT	סֻכּוֹת	3	good morning	BO-ker tov	בֹּקֶר טוֹב
6	braided bread	kha-LA	חַלָּה	3	good week	sha-VOO-a tov	שָׁבוּעַ טוֹב
5	bread	LE-khem	לֶחֶם	5	hallelujah	ha-l-loo-YA	הַלְלוּיָהּ
4	candle stick /lamp	m-no-RA	מְנוֹרָה	9	happy holiday	khag sa-ME-akh	חַג שָׂמֵחַ
8	charity	ts-da-KA	צְדָקָה	4	hear/listen	sh-MA	שְׁמַע
4	covenant	b-reet	בְּרִית	6	heart	lev	לֵב
9	clean/pure	ta-HOR	טָהוֹר	6	Hebrew	eev-REET	עִבְרִית
7	commandment	meets-VA	מִצְוָה	8	holy	ka-DOSH	קָדוֹשׁ
8	community/congregation	k-hee-LA	קְהִילָה	8	Holy Spirit	ROO-akh ha-KO-desh	רוּחַ הַקּוֹדֶשׁ
4	Dad/Daddy	A-ba	אַבָּא	8	honor/glory	ka-VOD	כָּבוֹד
1	daughter	bat	בַּת	8	Hope, the	ha-teek-VA	הַתִּקְוָה
6	David	da-VEED	דָּוִד	3	instruction	to-RA	תּוֹרָה
3	day	yom	יוֹם	9	Israel	yees-ra-EL	יִשְׂרָאֵל
8	Day of Atonement	yom kee-POOR	יוֹם כִּפּוּר	7	Jerusalem	y-roo-sha-LAI-yeem	יְרוּשָׁלַיִם
8	dedication, Feast of Dedication	kha-noo-KA	חֲנֻכָּה	9	joy	seem-KHA	שִׂמְחָה
9	doorpost, prayer box	m-zoo-ZA	מְזוּזָה	9	Joy of the Torah	seem-KHAT to-RA	שִׂמְחַת תּוֹרָה
8	everything's OK	ha-KOL b-SE-der	הַכֹּל בְּסֵדֶר	9	kindness	KHE-sed	חֶסֶד
8	everything	ha-KOL	הַכֹּל	5	king	ME-lekh	מֶלֶךְ
5	faith	e-moo-NA	אֱמוּנָה	5	knee	BE-rekh	בֶּרֶךְ
7	family	meesh-pa-KHA	מִשְׁפָּחָה	7	life	khai-YEEM	חַיִּים
6	father	av	אָב	4	light	or	אוֹר
6	friends	kha-ve-REEM	חֲבֵרִים	7	live	khai	חַי

Hebrew Dictionary (cont.)

Less #	English	Transliteration	Hebrew	Less #	English	Transliteration	Hebrew
3,5,6	LORD	a-do-NAI, ya, ye-ho-VA, ha-SHEM, Yahweh	יְהוָה, יָהּ, יְהֹוָה, יְיָ	7	son of (the) commandment	bar meets-VA	בַּר מִצְוָה
7	lots, Festival of Lots	poo-REEM	פּוּרִים	7	sons of	b-NAY	בְּנֵי
6	love - noun	a-ha-VA	אַהֲבָה	8	soul	**NE**-fesh	נֶפֶשׁ
9	love - FS verb	o-**HE**-vet	אוֹהֶבֶת	6	spirit, wind, breath	**ROO**-akh	רוּחַ
9	love - MS verb	o-HEV	אוֹהֵב	3	sun	**SHE**-mesh	שֶׁמֶשׁ
6	mercy/mercies	ra-kha-MEEM	רַחֲמִים	3	teacher - FS	mo-RA	מוֹרָה
3	Moses	**MO**-she	מֹשֶׁה	3	teacher - MS	mo-RE	מוֹרֶה
3	mountain	har	הַר	6	thanks	to-DA	תּוֹדָה
3	name	shem	שֵׁם	4	the comer, the one who comes	ha-BA	הַבָּא
6	Noah	**NO**-akh	נֹחַ	8	The Hope	ha-teek-VA	הַתִּקְוָה
9	order	**SE**-der	סֵדֶר	3	the Name	ha-SHEM	הַשֵׁם
7	our God	e-lo-**HAY**-noo	אֱלֹהֵינוּ	2	there	sham	שָׁם
9	Passover	**PE**-sakh	פֶּסַח	7	this/that	ze	זֶה
2	peace, hello, goodbye	sha-LOM	שָׁלוֹם	7	to life	l-khai-YEEM	לְחַיִּים
4	people	am	עַם	7	tree	ets	עֵץ
8	prayer	t-fee-LA	תְּפִלָּה	7	tree of life	ets khai-YEEM	עֵץ חַיִּים
9	prayer shawl	ta-LEET	טַלִּית	6	turn/return	shoov	שׁוּב
5	Rachel	ra-KHEL	רָחֵל	8	wedding canopy	khoo-PA	חֻפָּה
8	ram's horn	sho-FAR	שׁוֹפָר	6	weeks, Feast of Weeks, Pentecost	sha-voo-OT	שָׁבוּעוֹת
5	Ruth	root	רוּת	5	welcome - MS *Blessed is the one who comes*	ba-ROOKH ha-BA	בָּרוּךְ הַבָּא
1	Sabbath	sha-BAT	שַׁבָּת	5	welcome – plural *Blessed are those who come*	broo-KHEEM ha-ba-EEM	בְּרוּכִים הַבָּאִים
9	Sabbath Delight/meal on Sabbath	**O**-neg sha-BAT	עֹנֶג שַׁבָּת	3	what	ma	מָה
5	salvation	y-shoo-A	יְשׁוּעָה	6	work/serve/worship	a-vo-DA	עֲבוֹדָה
8	sanctification	kee-DOOSH	קִדּוּשׁ	9	worthy	ra-OO-ee	רָאוּי
4	see you later	l-hee-tra-OT	לְהִתְרָאוֹת	4	you - FS	at	אַתְּ
4	Solomon	**SHLO**-mo	שְׁלֹמֹה	4	you - MS	a-TA	אַתָּה
4	son	ben	בֵּן	6	Zion	tsee-YON	צִיּוֹן

Teacher Resources

Supply List

√	Item	Lesson
	3 X 5 notecards, lined or unlined	1
	Dreidel for show & tell	2
	2-4 fly swatters for Slap Game	2
	Print board game on colored card stock for each group	3
	Dice for board game – 1 die for every 2-4 people	3 & 7
	Game markers – different color for each person in a group	3
	Menorah for show and tell	4
	Print Tic-Tac-Toe on colored cardstock for each pair of students	4
	Make pieces (2 colors) for Tic-Tac-Toe– 5 of each color per pair	4
	Soft toy to throw for practicing phrases	5
	Print Self-quiz answer sheet – 1 per student	5
	Print Shalom Chaverim Pages – give each student 1 page	6
	Candy bar or other item to pass for phrase practice	7
	Prayer shawl to show tzitzits for show and tell	7
	Mezuzah for show and tell	7
	Hatikva recording	8
	Print & cut Memory Game on colored cardstock – for each pair	8
	Print & cut 2 copies on cardstock of Game page 1 and 2	9
	Print 1 copy of Praise Puzzle on colored cardstock	10
	Print Graduation certificates (in Teacher Resource section)	10
	Print copies of Post Quiz with answers - 1 per student	10

HWJ Teacher's Guide
Shalom Chaverim

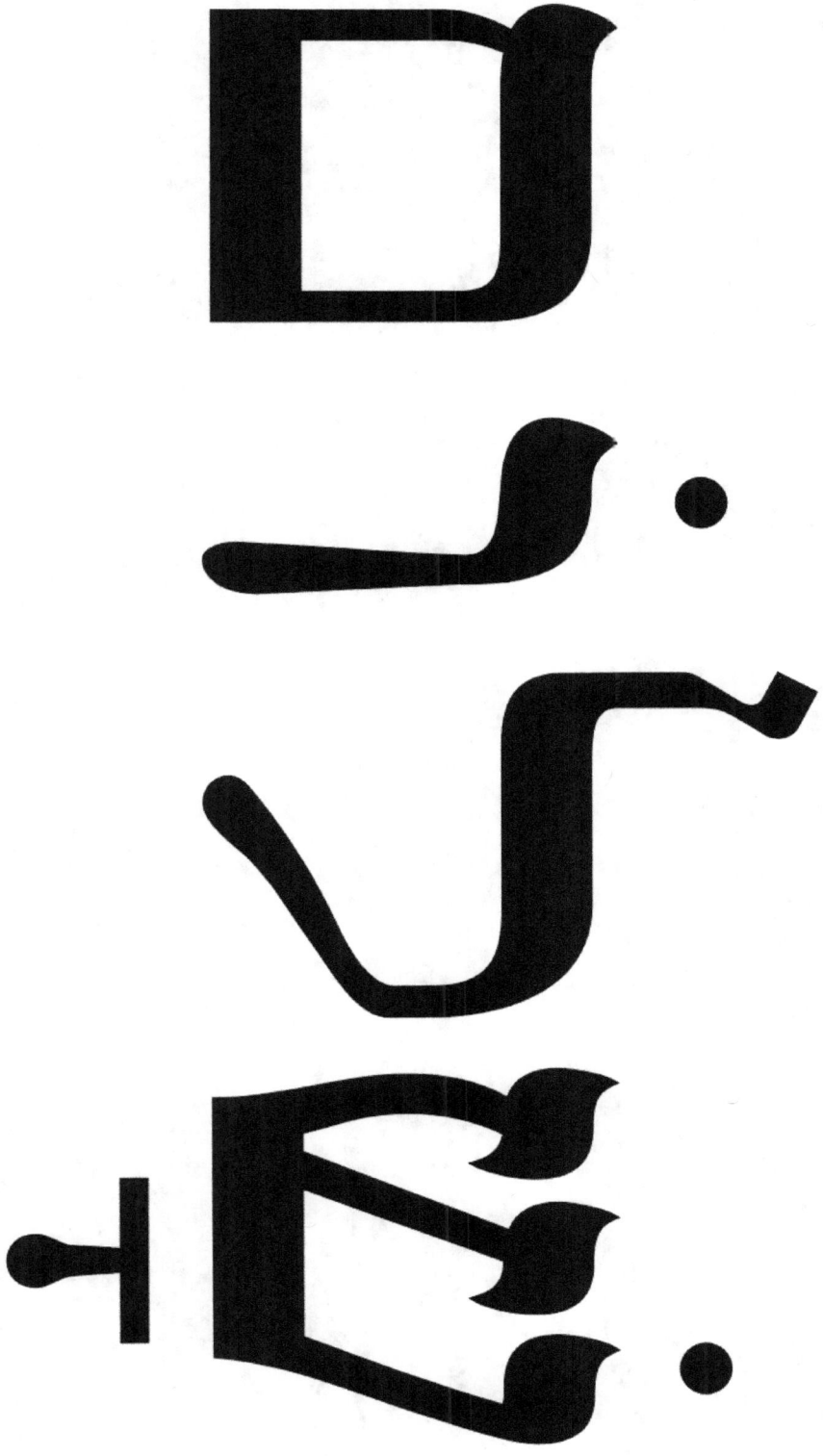

111

שָׁלוֹם חֲבֵרִים

HWJ Teacher's Guide
Shalom Chaverim

Teacher Resources

115

Hebrew with Joy!
Certificate of Graduation
מַזָל טוֹב!

שֵׁם: _____

Granted on: _____

Instructor: _____